Get Funded!

*A Definitive Guide to Seeking
the Right Funding, at the Right Time,
and from the Right Source*

Naeem Zafar

*Haas Business School,
University of California, Berkeley*

www.Startup-Advisor.com

Get Funded!
A Definitive Guide to Seeking the Right Funding, at the Right Time, from the Right Source

Copyright © 2010 by Naeem Zafar

Published by:

Five Mountain Press
Cupertino, California USA
info@FiveMountainPress.com
www.FiveMountainPress.com

ISBN 13: 978-0-9823420-6-0
ISBN 10: 0-9823420-6-3
Printed in the United States of America

Table of Contents

Why I Wrote This Book..5

How to Use This Book..9

Three Main Sections..11

    Section I: Know Your Options..11

    Section II: Prepare Yourself for Seeking Funding................13

    Section III: The Funding Process..13

SECTION 1: KNOW YOUR OPTIONS..................................15

    Chapter 1: The Entrepreneur's Sources of Funding........17

        Types of Investors..18

        Six Funding Stages for Your Company................................20

        Bootstrapping...21

        FFF: Friends, Family & Fools..26

        Government Grants and Loans..28

        The Next Stage: Professional Investors..............................31

        Seed-Stage Investors...33

        Early-Stage to Mid-Stage Venture Capitalists (VCs)........35

        Late-Stage Options...36

        Strategic Investors..36

        Summary..37

    Chapter 2: The Investors' Profiles....................................41

        Friends & Family..42

        Angel Investors..48

        Why Angels Invest...49

        Venture Capitalists (VCs)..51

        Banks..54

        Venture Debt..54

        Strategic Investors..59

Chapter 3: The Secret World of Venture Capitalists................63

Where Do VCs Get Their Money?................67

The VC Model................67

How Do VCs Make Money?................69

Limited Partners (LPs)................72

How VCs Invest the LPs' Money................75

Discover a VC Fund's Focus................78

The Anatomy of a VC Firm................79

What are Your Odds of Being Funded by a VC?................84

The Profile of a VC................86

Inside Structure of a VC Firm................87

EIR Programs................90

How VCs Evaluate a Company................91

Syndication................92

Chapter 4: Investors' Motivations and Your Funding Strategy................97

Why Angel Investors Invest................97

Why VCs Invest................98

VCs' Investment Criteria................101

VC Firm Size and Tiers................103

Why Do Strategic Investors Invest?................106

Your Investment Strategy................106

SECTION 2: PREPARE YOURSELF FOR SEEKING FUNDING................109

Chapter 5: How to Get Investor-Ready: A Must-Do Checklist................113

Market Validation and the Unmet Need................117

Market Traction Proof Point................118

Target Customers and Market Size................121

Competitive Landscape................122

Business Model................123

Financial Assumptions................123

Sensitivity Analysis and "What if" Scenarios................125

Key Performance Indicators (KPIs) and Financial Projections........125

The Team..129

Chapter 6: Approaching and Engaging Investors................135

The Art of Networking..137

Presenting Your Company to the VCs..141

What Is in an Executive Summary?..141

VC Meeting & Presentation Preparation...144

Tips for Presenting to Investors..147

Presentation Style...150

Slide Zero...153

SECTION 3: THE FUNDING PROCESS..155

Chapter 7: The 12-Step Process of Getting Funded...............157

The Process..158

Get Referred..160

What Do You Need to Send Investors?...161

Fine-Tune Your Message...163

Approach Investors in Stages...165

You, Under Scrutiny...167

The Due Diligence Phase..170

Term Sheet...175

How Do You Know You Are Seeing Interest from VCs?......................178

The Closing..180

Chapter 8: A Primer on Term Sheets...................................183

Common vs. Preferred Shares...185

Stages of Funding...186

1. Valuation...187

Aim for an "Up Round"..189

The Down Round...190

2. Exit Math: Who Gets What in an Exit Scenario.............................191

Liquidation Preferences 193

3. Governance...195

4. Founder's Treatment...198

Termination With Cause...201

Constructive Termination..202

Change in Control..202

How to Negotiate a Term Sheet..................................204

Don't Over-Negotiate; Be Professional.....................207

Chapter 9: Post-funding Priorities...........................209

Running Your Company..209

Extend Your Lifeline!..210

Board Relationship and Management........................211

How Often to Approach Board Members..................212

Running Board Meetings..213

Chapter 10: What If You Don't Get Funded?............215

Are You Doomed?..217

Alternatives..218

Technology or Company Sale.......................................220

Chapter 11: Final Advice...223

APPENDICES..227

Example of an Executive Summary Template from

www.bandangels.com...228

Resources for Entrepreneurs.......................................229

List of VCs...231

List of Angel Investors..236

NAEEM ZAFAR..239

Why I Wrote This Book

It was the last Friday of the month and Jacob was getting his hair cut again, a routine that he had kept for the last seven years. During the normal process of filling his barber in on his life between shampoo and trim, Jacob ended up talking with him about how a bunch of people—myself included—were giving up our day jobs to start a new company. As it turned out, this barber also cut the hair of Dean Scheff, the CEO of CPT Corporation. CPT Corporation was a pioneer in the word processing business that had gone public. (Mind you, this was in 1985 and there was no Microsoft Word yet.) Dean, himself, was an entrepreneur and understood what it takes to start and grow a company. This useful connection resulted in Dean and Jacob meeting. A few weeks later, CPT Corporation invested $500,000 in seed capital, and our company, XCAT, was started for the purpose of making a specialized computer that was expected to accelerate scientific computation by six orders of magnitude.

We had connected with the right investor at the right time and had sought the right funding. This funding allowed our company to develop our first prototype and get our first customer. The VC money followed.

In this book I will outline all that I have learned about getting startups funded as an entrepreneur, as an investor, and as an educator on this topic.

Most entrepreneurs think they need to meet an investor as soon as they have an idea, but this is the wrong way to go about it. Before you meet with investors, you must become "investor-ready." What does this mean, how does one become investor-ready, and who are these investors? In this book, I will answer these questions and more.

Funding is the one thing that is foremost in the mind of almost every entrepreneur. In reality, it should not be one's focus, but it is. Instead, many other things should be the focus of your attention:

- knowing your ideal target market;
- creating a product that you know provides solutions for your customers, based on

research you've done with the customers themselves;

♦ putting the right team in place;

♦ and preparing an executable plan.

Once you have accomplished all of these things, the funding will come to you. I know, having been there myself, that this is NOT how a first-time entrepreneur thinks, however. Instead, he or she thinks, "I could conquer all aspects of starting a new venture IF ONLY I had access to funds!"

I hope this book will enlighten entrepreneurs on all aspects of funding, including when to seek it, from whom to seek it, and how to find it. This process is often a mystery to entrepreneurs, so they approach investors, or people who look like investors, ill prepared and at the wrong time. Worst of all, they don't understand the reasoning or mindset of the investors they approach. As a result, a lot of time and effort is wasted, frustration sets in, and many good ideas are lost. It is my intention to help educate you on the proper process of attaining funding for your startup business. I want you to be very informed so you will seek the right funding, from the right source, at the right time. When you do that, you will be much more likely to get the funding you need!

I have been an entrepreneur almost all my life and have raised tens of millions of dollars from venture capitalists, angel investors, strategic investors, and bank financing, as well as from friends and family. When one is seeking funds, each of these sources requires a different mindset. My intention in this book is to demystify these processes so that you can successfully navigate the choppy waters of funding.

How to Use This Book

Every company, at each stage in its life, will need capital to grow; every entrepreneur has to learn how to deal with fundraising for his or her startup company; and at each stage of a company's development, its money-raising options change.

There are different opportunities available to a startup for raising money. In Chapter 2, we will look at the different kinds of investors out there. I will teach you how to determine which type you should approach, based primarily on which stage of growth your company is in. Then, I will show you how to approach investors in a way that maximizes your chance of success.

The chart below represents a typical cash balance of a startup business. You need to be clear about this diagram, which reveals a lot more than you may think. It tells an investor how much cash you will need in order to turn the corner on profitability, how long it will take you to become profitable, and what the outcome will be a few years down the road in terms of revenue and profits. This information provides the investor with a basis for making a decision to invest in your venture.

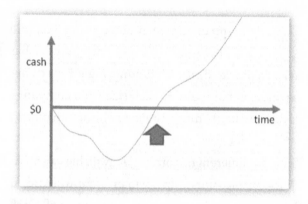

Suppose this chart shows your company's income. It is negative at the start of the business, showing how much cash you will burn before you turn the cash flow positive (1), how long it will be before you turn it positive, and what your "run rate" (how much will you be making per month that your revenue exceeds your expenses) will be when you turn that corner. These three items should be on the tip of your tongue.

Three Main Sections

I have organized this book into three main sections based on the three key stages of getting funding for your company. First, you have to know your options for getting funded, then, how one prepares himself or herself for seeking funding, and finally, what the actual process of getting the funding involves.

Section I: Know Your Options

Section I deals with understanding funding options. There are many different sources of funding, and it is vital that you understand these various types of investors and their mindsets. Why do they invest? What do they look for in potential investments (since each investor type has a different set of criteria)? And where can you find these investors?

In any endeavor of life, the best thing you can do to ensure success is educate yourself. This is especially true when you are seeking funding for your startup company. You need to know the following things about your potential investors:

- Who are these investors?
- What forms and shapes do they come in (angel investors, angel groups, venture capitalists, or strategic investors)?
- Why should they be interested in you?
- What data do they look for while making an investment decision?
- What gets them excited?
- How can you get introduced to the right investors?
- How should you approach them?
- What should you say when you meet with them?

There may be scores of questions, including the ones above, floating through your mind. In this section, I try to answer most of them in the most logical order.

Section II: Prepare Yourself for Seeking Funding

Section II deals with you, the entrepreneur, and how you can get investor ready. It's essential that you understand the proper method and timing for approaching investors. I strongly suggest that you not approach investors until you are truly ready to do so. Each investor type requires different preparation. We will discuss these types of preparation in detail in this section.

Section III: The Funding Process

Section III deals with the process of getting funded. How do you negotiate with these investors? What is negotiable and what is not? What happens if you <u>do</u> get funded, and what is expected of you? Even more importantly, what happens if you do <u>not</u> get the right funding? Not every company is ready to seek funding from every source available, and each stage of company growth dictates the best choice of investment. So, given where your company is, what options do you really have?

In this book, I am summarizing my 25 years as an entrepreneur. I've spent years raising money, and I've hung out with investors and venture capitalists. I've advised hundreds of entrepreneurs and helped them raise millions of dollars. My experience gives me some knowledge and perspective that you should find useful. (You can find out more about my experience by looking at my bio at the end of the book.)

My style is direct and no-nonsense. I will tell you exactly what I know and believe about getting funded. But I don't want you to think that there is only one way to get money. There are actually hundreds of ways! Even if you don't follow all of my suggestions, you will find knowledge in this e-book that will help you do a better job of raising money and dealing with investors.

SECTION I

Know Your Options

Should an entrepreneur approach venture capitalists (VCs) or angel investors? Where does one find these investors? What would make them want to talk to someone? Should an entrepreneur approach a bank, or raise money from friends and family? These are the types of questions all entrepreneurs have on their minds when thinking about funding their startups.

In this section, I will help you understand the kinds of investors that are out there. I will profile them for you. It's almost certain that you will interact with one or more of these types of investors over the life of your company. Whom you interact with will be based on the nature of your business and the stage your business is in. A company's funding needs change over time, so at each stage of a company's growth, a different type of investor is needed.

In this first section, I will help you understand who these investor types are and why they invest. I'll describe to you how they make money. Understanding their profiles and motivations will help you approach them correctly. This greatly increases your probability of success once you contact them.

In Sections 2 and 3, I will cover the other main topics: being investor-ready and the process of getting funded.

CHAPTER 1

The Entrepreneur's Sources of Funding

I mentioned at the start of this book that my first startup company was able to get seed funding (just over $500,000), thanks to a barber! Yes, indeed. Four of us were starting a company that was to design and sell specialized computers called hardware accelerators. My barber made the connection between his two clients, and the CEO of CPT, Dean Scheff, became our first angel investor. Our company, XCAT, was launched in a suburb of Minneapolis in 1985 in a vacated warehouse that CPT owned, and it went on to raise venture capital money within a few years. Investors come in all sizes and forms, and it is important for entrepreneurs to understand their options. As their ventures grow, they will need to approach different types of investors.

Types of Investors

Once you have convinced yourself that your business can make money, you will be able to convince others that they can make money from your business too. Investors come in two basic shapes: people who want to see you succeed and are willing to help you, and people who want to help you in order to make money for themselves.

The first category includes your friends and family, as well as some government grants, such as Small Business Investment Research (SBIR) grants. The second category includes angel investors, venture capitalists, banks, and strategic investors. No matter which category they fall into, every investor has different motives for investing. Whether you should use one category or the other, or possibly both, is based on the stage your business is in. A growing and successful venture will use sources from both categories during the course of its life cycle. I, myself, have used all of them in my businesses.

Why investors invest

Simply put, investors want a superior return on their money. The question is, how will they know that your idea has merit? After all, they are unlikely to understand your business as well as you do. One of the main things that professional investors need to see is whether or not there is "traction" in your business. Traction occurs when your message is connecting with your customers, who then provide clear signs of their willingness to purchase. It describes, in a single word, the most important criteria for investment.

This is why you go through bootstrapping your business and seeking money from your friends and family (as well as other people in the first category that I define above). You do it simply to demonstrate that there is traction. <u>Traction is the proof that your customers are buying (or willing to buy) your product</u>. Having consumers making a commitment, for example, that if you had this product available today, they would buy it proves that your business has traction, which, in turn, attracts investors to you.

Six Funding Stages for Your Company

As I said before, the type of investors you will be approaching depends on the stage of growth your business is in. The figure below illustrates six growth stages. It shows that different amounts of capital are needed in each stage, capital that will likely come from different sources.

As you start your business, it will go through these various stages. Each stage has different dynamics and needs; hence, the sources of funding must change. When you first have an idea (assuming that you are not famous yet!), the most likely option will be to fund this exploration phase yourself until you can demonstrate that your idea has merit and can make money for your investors. If you have already started and successfully concluded a business or two and are thus already famous, then people will be willing to give you money simply due to your reputation. The funny thing is, if you had previously demonstrated success, you probably would not need other people's money. So, here is your first lesson of funding: it is much easier to raise money when you don't actually need it! Remember this lesson; you will come back to it later in this book and throughout your entrepreneurial life.

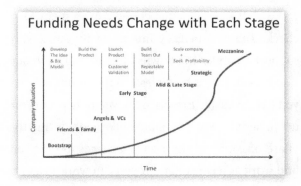

Funding Needs Change with Each Stage

Bootstrapping

The first stage is called the bootstrapping phase. Boot-strapping means applying your own savings to shape an idea and build your product or service. In this stage, you are still trying to prove to your-self that there is a business here worth pursuing, and it is unlikely that any investor will give you money during this stage. Perhaps, you'll be able to convince your mom to provide you with some capital. Other than that, however, it's your savings, your credit card, and maybe some loans you take against your personal assets that go towards your startup.

For many of you, the money may come from the job that you are working in addition to the work you are doing on your startup. Having a steady job provides you with the security that comes from a steady pay-check. This is especially important if you need to support a family. The downside of having a job out-side your startup is that it lessens the amount of time you have available to work on developing your prod-uct or service. So, if you must take a job during this phase of your startup, I have a suggestion for you: find work as a consultant. If you can work as a con-sultant in the field of the product you are develop-ing, you can earn a living and gain valuable insights about your customers at the same time. Once you have your product on the market, you may be able to turn some of your consulting clients into customers for your startup. Whether you have another job or not, remember that during the bootstrapping phase, you are researching the viability of your company, and you want to do this research as frugally as pos-sible. (I describe this stage of bootstrapping and dis-covery in more detail in my e-book *Market Research on a Shoestring*, which you can purchase at the fol-lowing website: www.FiveMountainPress.com.)

The frugal mindset

Bootstrapping is also a mindset. It makes you think and act differently from how you would if your current employer had assigned you to a project. When your own money is on the line, you are forced to ask many questions about whether or not you really want to spend money doing this right now. This mindset creates a culture of smart frugality and creativeness that will serve you well as an entrepreneur. Investors like this too. It shows them that you will be smart with <u>their</u> money once they invest.

There are three main reasons to bootstrap:

1) In order to make sure your idea has merit before you take money from any investor, even friends and family, as you do not want to jeopardize those relationships.

2) Because your investors will have a much higher level of confidence in you knowing that you have put your own money into an idea.

3) Because the value of your company increases as you work to solidify the idea and your business plan, i.e., when you raise money from investors, it will be at a higher valua-

tion. Thus, you will part with less equity in
your efforts to attract investors (meaning,
you will keep more of your company).

Bootstrapping is certainly attractive, as it allows
you to give away less of your company and enjoy a
bigger piece of ownership. At some point, you will
probably use banks as your source of necessary
funding to run the operations of your business. But
because most startups do not have any assets early
on and banks will want some collateral in return,
your startup will not be able to attract banks as a
source of its capital. Of course, you can get a bank
loan if you put down your personal assets as collateral, but I advise you not to invest a lot of capital
in your business until you have done the market
research and are fairly certain that your business
idea can be successful.

Why Stop Bootstrapping?

Bootstrapping all the way is good if you can af-
ford to do it. But often, the speed of execution
that is needed makes it hard <u>not</u> to seek investors.
Investors such as VCs and angels can help accelerate growth and shorten the time to market. Speed
is usually a key factor in gaining market share.

If you can grow your business to the profitability stage without using professional investors, go for it. But do not underestimate the value of the acceleration that comes with not having to bootstrap all the time. Another benefit that comes from being involved with professional investors is the guidance and advice they can provide—if you choose them wisely! These investors have years, maybe even decades, of experience and can give you insight into your business that is hard to find anywhere else.

How Long to Bootstrap?

How much capital do you need during this bootstrapping phase? It depends on your product and your level of frugality, but usually, you will need anywhere from a few hundred to a few thousand dollars. All investors will expect you to contribute some of your own money to the bootstrapping phase of your startup. They figure that if you are not willing to put your own money into discovering whether or not your idea is worth pursuing, then maybe you don't believe in the idea that much. They take it as a sign that you are the wrong person to invest a great deal of money in!

Once you have gone through the bootstrapping phase and you have successfully passed through at least one proof point, then you are likely to attract an investor. This proof point can come in many different forms: a mock-up of a website, a beta version of your product, or very detailed product specifications.

After establishing an initial proof point, you may be ready to start thinking about who can provide capital for the next phase of your company. The more proof points you establish, the easier it becomes to attract investors. It is not uncommon for investors to expect (or even insist) that you have actual revenue and several thousand users for a web-based business.

FFF: Friends, Family & Fools

Once you are fairly certain that your idea holds a strong potential for business and you have completed most of the 7-step process of discovery (described in my e-book of the same name, available on   www.FiveMountainPress.com/books.html), then you are ready to approach people in the "FFF" category. This is the stage when you go to friends, family, and fools. (I use the term "fools" in a joking manner, simply because these people aren't investing out of a deep conviction that the product will be successful, as I'm about to show.)

People in this category don't necessarily give you money because they understand your idea or believe in the investment thesis. They give because they believe in <u>you</u>. They believe in your dedication, and they are willing to invest some money in order to see you become successful.

Pros and cons of using friends and family

There are some real advantages to getting money from friends and family. One of the chief advantages is that you already know these people. Furthermore, they know you, they believe in you, and they trust you. You don't have to establish credibility with them. Since they are giving you money because of their relationship with you, they should not be as upset as other investors if your startup fails and they lose money.

One disadvantage you may want to consider, however, is that when you take money from friends and family, you are mixing your business life with your personal life. Before accepting money from a friend or a relative, you should ask yourself, "If I take money from this person and the startup doesn't succeed, will it damage our relationship?"

Pros and cons of using friends and family continued

It can be really awkward during holiday get-togethers if your entire family is angry with you about the money you lost. Be sure that the friends and family members who are providing you with funding won't hold it against you if things don't work out for your business.

Government Grants and Loans

Almost every country has some sort of program to help entrepreneurs. The U.S. Small Business Administration (SBA) Office of Technology administers loan guarantees for small business startups, and almost every federal government agency provides grants under the Small Business Innovation Research (SBIR) and the Small Business Technology Transfer (STTR) programs. Through these two competitive programs, governmental agencies (from NASA to the Department of Energy and many others in between) ensure that the nation's small, innovative high-tech businesses represent a significant part of the federal government's research and development efforts. Eleven government departments participate in the SBIR program, and five departments participate in the STTR program, together awarding $2 billion to small high-tech businesses.

What is SBA?

The U.S. Small Business Administration (SBA) was created in 1953 as an independent agency of the federal government to aid, counsel, assist, and protect the interests of small businesses; to preserve free, competitive enterprise; and to maintain and strengthen the overall economy of the United States. SBA helps by providing loan guarantees and some venture capital through a partnership with SBIC (Small Business Investment Company). More information is available on www.SBA.gov.

While the SBA is also a source of loans for small businesses, SBIR grants are not loans; they are grants. Each department of the U.S. government has a portion of the federal budget allocated to it for the SBIR grants that it provides. The process for obtaining such grants is long and burdened with bureaucracy, you must fill out many forms to apply, and it can take four to six months to get your first grant; but in a Phase One SBIR grant, it's possible to get an amount ranging from $50,000 to $100,000.

Any intellectual property developed under this grant is owned by the U.S. government.

Furthermore, the entire process of applying for and receiving this grant takes longer than most entrepreneurs would want to wait to get started. Nevertheless, it is a source of funding that should not be ignored. For many entrepreneurs, finding the right government department and applying for such a grant may be a fine way to start.

Check out http://www.sbir.gov/ and http://www.grants.gov/ for more information on these options. The U.S National Science Foundation administers the SBIR site on behalf of the federal government. Each government department website can be searched for additional information on these grants. For example, check out http://sbir.nasa.gov/ to find out more about grants given by NASA.

The Next Stage: Professional Investors

Once you have achieved some market traction, which ideally consists of actual customers parting with their money to buy your product or service (more on this in Section 3), then you can approach real investors. (As I said earlier, traction can also mean you have sufficient proof that customers would be willing to part with their money if you had your product available for them to purchase.) You will need to put in some serious work in order to be ready to approach professional investors. You must walk into investor meetings having done significant research in your go-to-market strategies and having demonstrated your ability to put a team together in order to execute a business plan (more on this in Chapter 5).

Professional investors come in the form of angel investors, early-stage or seed-stage venture capitalists, and firms that specifically provide "seed funding." At this stage, businesses usually start with angel investors and try to raise anywhere from one hundred thousand to a million dollars. This allows them to demonstrate further traction and proof points before they begin to talk to venture capitalists.

When bypassing angels makes sense

In a small percentage of cases, angel, or seed-stage, investors can be bypassed for the venture capitalists. For example, if your ideas have great potential or require larger sums of money then what angels are capable of coming up with, the people involved have a reputation of being brilliant, or the VC had looked at the idea before but hadn't been able to find the right team, then you may be able to skip the early funding stages and engage a VC earlier. In general, however, the proper sequence of events includes involving angel investors or bootstrapping to the point of sufficient traction first and then contacting the VCs. In general, I warn entrepreneurs that it is foolish to start approaching investors until they have done sufficient research and preparation and can demonstrate successful proof points and market traction.

Seed-Stage Investors

Once you have done your homework and started creating market traction, you should start searching for angel investors. Also known as seed-stage investors, they are more likely than other investors to recognize the hope, excitement, and energy in you that they once saw in themselves. They may be the right source of a relatively small amount of funding (from $50,000 to $1 million).

The criteria that angel investors use to evaluate potential investments are often less analytical and a bit more emotional. They may be inclined to base their decisions to work with you on the simple fact that they like you. This is different from professional VCs, who will have a pretty standard set of criteria to follow in order to determine whether or not they will invest in your startup.

Many angels will form a group and act as a group to source deals, evaluate them, and then decide whether or not to invest in them. Examples of such angel funds in the Silicon Valley include The Band of Angels (http://www.bandangels.com/), Sandhill Angels (http://www.sandhillangels.com/), and the Angel's Forum (http://www.angelsforum.com/).

Some firms like to work with bright entrepreneurs even if those entrepreneurs lack the kind of track record that VCs usually look for. They may invest a small amount in your business if they like the space (or domain) that you are working in. If they see the market potential of what you are doing and believe you will need a bigger round of capital in the near future, they may provide this small invest-ment along with an expectation to provide addi-tional funding. These investment vehicles are often known as "seed funds."

Examples of seed funds that provide a small amount of early funding for select entrepreneurs include XSEED (at http://www.xseedcap.com/) and Y-Combinator (at http://ycombinator.com/). Check out the Y-Combinator website for more de-tails on this very popular model of investors pro-viding seed-stage entrepreneurs with very small amounts of funding (between $10K to $15K) to seed their companies. This money provides mini-mal funding for only three months, but often it is just enough to help you get started and get some recognition. Several interesting startups have come out of this type of seed funding.

Early-Stage to Mid-Stage Venture Capitalists (VCs)

In an upcoming chapter, I will describe in greater detail the various types of investors and their investment motivation. For now, it's enough to know that VCs are part of professional organizations that raise money from institutions in order to invest in startups.

VC firms come in dozens of shapes and forms. Some like to invest in particular industries, such as medical devices, internet software, or internet infrastructure. Some focus on early-stage companies, others on mid-stage companies, and yet others on late-stage companies. This diversity in focus results in differing investment criteria and specialties. It means that different VC firms will have varying levels of patience with you, and they will regard different issues as being of paramount importance. As a result, there is no "one-size-fits-all" approach to seeking VC funding. You really have to do your homework so you know which VC is most likely to want to fund your project.

Late-Stage Options

As your venture matures, new options will open up
to you. Once you have significant VCs with deep
pockets behind you, commercial banks will start
showing an interest in you. They will want to open
up lines of credit for you, so that you can borrow
large amounts of money from them. This will en-
able you to make your business grow faster. These
options also come with significant risks, however.
We will discuss their pros and cons later.

Strategic Investors

Once you have carved out significant traction or
promise, strategic investors may start to show
interest. These investors are companies that can
benefit from your assets. Some of these companies may be interested in investing in you in order
to gain new technology and will hope to gain the
right to purchase or license your product or service
in the future. Some may be interested in acquiring your customer base or geographic reach. If, for
example, you have one million users in Brazil, a
web-based company that operates only in Mexico
and Argentina may find your Brazilian presence
very attractive. It may want to invest in you so it
may gain knowledge about the Brazilian market.

Perhaps someday, it may even want to acquire your company.

Large companies often have a corporate investment group—an internal group that has the task of scouting for new and interesting technologies that can benefit the large company. Its job is to keep an eye out for other companies that may provide attractive investments, either for the purpose of acquisition or so that they may be kept out of the hands of competitors. Intel, Google, Facebook, and Genentech are all strategic investors that have such groups.

Summary

Hopefully, you can see from this overview that investors are not just one big monolith. There are dozens of different types of investors who provide dozens of options for your startup. Your decision as to which types to pursue should be based on what you are trying to accomplish and what stage your venture is in. We will take a closer look at each of these options later in the book.

The following chart shows the typical funding stages that a company goes through and the kinds of activity that a company is engaged in at each stage:

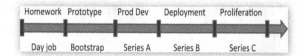

Series A, B, and C refer to subsequent rounds of funding by VCs. Each timeshare of the company is issued to investors. Each of these shares is identified by a new series number. This chart outlines the various stages of company growth. You must be sure to approach the right investor for each stage. Approaching VCs before you have any traction will be a waste of time for you and for them. It is important to realize that as your company moves to a new stage, it will require more capital and your choices of potential investors should be clearer to you.

It is possible that you can bootstrap a company to revenue and profitability, thereby eliminating the need for angels or VCs. Many companies have been created this way, and you may find that this is the best avenue for your startup. Many other startups, however, find that in order to succeed, they need outside funding. One general rule to follow is this: get as little funding as you need in order to be successful. While it's very nice to have inves-

tor's money to spend, remember that every dollar you get from an investor costs you something
in return. Usually, that cost is ownership in your
startup.

Not All Great Companies Were VC Funded:

- **Broadcom**: No VC money
- **Cisco**: $5M in revenue, profitable before Sequoia invested
- **Dell**: Raised money at $60M in revenue
- **eBay**: $4.5M in revenue and profitable before Benchmark invested
- **Microsoft**: VC funded after being profitable
- **The MathWorks** – more than $300M in revenue, no VC money
- **Oracle**: Government contract funded first product
- **SAS Institute**: $1.9B in revenue, the largest private software company, no VC money
- **Siebel**: Customers funded first product

With that being said, let's go on. Let's look at the different types of investors you are likely to encounter.
What makes them tick? What do they expect from
you? I will answer these and other questions in
Chapter 2.

The Investors' Profiles

What are the types of investors most likely to consider providing funding for your company, and why would they want to invest in you? Let's analyze each type individually.

There are five different types of investors you are likely to see:

1) Friends and family
2) Angel investors
3) VCs
4) Bankers
5) Strategic investors

Chances are you will interact with all of them at various times during the growth of your startup. As discussed in the previous chapter, after you have bootstrapped, the most common source of funding will be friends and family. This sort of funding can take you to the point where you have some validation of your ideas.

Friends & Family

Your friends and members of the family usually invest because they believe that you will do the right thing with your business. Sometimes, they just want to be supportive. The amount of money you can raise through friends and family depends on what kinds of friends and what kind of family you have. Commonly, I see people raising anywhere from ten thousand to a couple hundred thousand dollars through this means.

This is a crucial stage—you need to use this money to get sufficient market traction. Real investors, which will come later, will give you money only after you have demonstrated sufficient market traction (a proof point that customers are willing to spend money to buy your product or service). The only exception to this is if you are very famous and your reputation alone as a money-making entrepreneur attracts them to bet on you. If you are already well known for startups you have created previously, some investors may be willing to invest in you at the very beginning of this one. Due to your reputation, they may trust that you will figure things out as you go. Typically, however, investors want to see market traction.

Usually, it is smarter to accept money from your friends and family in the form of a convertible debt than to issue them shares of your company. A convertible debt (also known as a convertible loan or note) is a loan that can be converted into shares of stock at a later date.

The magic of a convertible note

There are two ways to raise money from investors: you can take the money as a loan or you can sell equity (i.e., stock) in your company to them. Selling stock has the problem that both parties have to agree on what the company is "worth" in order to determine if a $50,000 investment gets a 5% stake in your venture or 10% or even 50%. Arriving at a value requires some rigorous calculations that typically only professional investors can handle.

There are two ways to raise money from investors: you can take the money as a loan or you can sell equity (i.e., stock) in your company to them.

The magic of a convertible note
continued

Selling stock has the problem that both parties have to agree on what the company is "worth" in order to determine if a $50,000 investment gets a 5% stake in your venture or 10% or even 50%. Arriving at a value requires some rigorous calculations that typically only professional investors can handle.

Another common way to raise money is by getting a loan that converts into equity when a professional investor establishes a value for your company. This is called a "convertible note." It is a loan from early- stage investors that is secured by the intellectual property and physical assets of the new company (if there are any). This loan converts to equity (stock) at some future round of investment.

In order to compensate for these investors having taken additional risks by investing in the startup so early, it is common to give them some "sweetener." This can take the form of their getting additional shares and, in some cases, accrued interest.

It is not uncommon to see such early investors get a 20% premium when they convert their debt into equity; i.e., because they invested early, they get 20% more shares than they otherwise would have been able to.

The magic of a convertible note
continued

In some cases, these early investors earn a small annual interest, comparable to what they would have earned by keeping the money they invested in some bank account. A figure of 5% to 8% per year is not uncommon for interest on these investments.

For example, let's assume that you raised $50,000 from friends in January. You used this money to get your website up and running, and by October, you started to generate significant traffic and developed a compelling business plan. You started to attract investors and were closing a Series A round of venture capital in December. When this round closes and your company issues new shares to the investors, you should also issue shares to your friends at the same price as they were issued to the investors and at the same terms and conditions. Due to a 10% interest on that original $50,000 and a 20% premium, the calculations would appear as if your friends invested $65,000 (and not the original $50,000), with $5,000 coming from one year's worth of interest and $10,000 from the risk premium of 20% on the original $50,000.

Issuing company shares early on leads to too many shareholders. This makes a company appear unattractive to professional investors or VCs. It is for this reason that you want to accept funding from friends and family as loans against the intellectual property of the company or the business itself. When you raise money from professional investors, the people who gave you early money will get shares at the price other investors get, plus a premium for investing early. The premium can be anywhere from 12% to 30%, meaning they get additional shares, above the amount generally earned for the capital they have contributed (see sidebar).

Separate your finances early!

You should set up a separate bank account for your new company as early as possible. If you have not formed the company yet, i.e., you have not gone through the legal expense of doing the formation ("formation" is legal speak for setting up a "company"), you can still set yourself up as a DBA ("Doing Business As"). Being a DBA allows you to assume a business name legally and to open an account and have checks with that business's name while it is just you behind the scene.

Separate your finances early!
continued

This is a common way small businesses conduct themselves in the United States. You can do this by filing papers with the county where you are starting your business. These county forms, which have different names depending on where you are, allow you to do business as an individual under a business name.

Suppose your name is Bill Johnson, and you are going to start a business delivering medications to the elderly at their homes. You want to setup a business called "MedCo Delivery." As a DBA, however, your business will officially be called, "Bill Johnson doing business as MedCo Delivery." The main reason you want to do this is because it allows you to open a bank account under MedCo Delivery. You may then receive checks and investment amounts from people without having to deposit them into your personal bank accounts.

It's also true that when you are ready to accept money from people, it's a good time to talk to a lawyer. You need to set up a legal entity to avoid liability. I discuss this subject in much more detail in my e-book The Entrepreneur's Legal Guide to Starting Up, which is also available at www.fivemountainpress.com.

Angel Investors

The second kind of investor is the angel investor. Angel investors are wealthy individuals who often were entrepreneurs themselves at some point in their lives and who enjoy interacting with young entrepreneurs. They tend to take some amount of their wealth and dabble in a few startups. In the United States, more companies are funded through angel investors than through venture capitalists, and these angel investors invest between $25 billion and $50 billion every year.

The problem is that it can be hard to find angel investors. It's not always clear where they are, or how to find them. In many cities, angel investors come together so they can act as a group. There are also several resources that can be used to find angel investors:

- ◆ Group meetings where entrepreneurs hang out. In Silicon Valley they will be VLAB events, such as those of MIT and Stanford Venture Labs, or various "MeetUp" groups.
- ◆ Alumni groups from various universities. MIT, Stanford, Cornell, and Brown all have active alumni networks in most major cities.

- ◆ Organizations, such as TIE (www.tie.org) and OPEN (www.OPENSiliconValley.org), that cater to entrepreneurs and offer events, education, and mentorship.

- ◆ Mailing lists and blogs, such as TechCrunch (http://techcrunch.com), and online networks of entrepreneurs, such as EFACTOR (www.efactor.com).

Angel groups

In Silicon Valley, there are five groups of angel investors that I know of: the Band of Angels, the Keiretsu Forum, the Sand Hill Angels, the Angel's Forum (TAF), and the Plug and Play Angels. These groups are unique because you can contact them directly and arrange to present your idea. Many angel investors are not as public. This is why you are more likely to find angels through other entrepreneurs or events where entrepreneurs hang out.

Why Angels Invest

Angels would usually choose to invest in your startup for two reasons. The first reason angels would invest in your startup is because you remind them of themselves at a younger age, when they were full of ideas and enthusiasm, and they take

a personal liking to you. The second possible reason is they love the area in which you are starting
your company, perhaps because they used to work
in that industry themselves. Suppose, for example,
the potential investor was once an executive in
the trucking industry and you have come up with
software that optimizes how trucks travel, helping
them save on gasoline. Since your service is in the
same industry in which the angel investor once
worked, he will be very excited about your efforts
to solve a problem that he probably dealt with at
some point in his career.

Angels can be Mentors
You must understand this point: Most of the time,
though not always, the reasons angel investors give
for funding you are emotional. It's either about you
or the domain you are working in. You must respect this, and you should feed on it. You also want
to extract value from these investors because they
probably will have a lot of knowledge about the
area of your work. An angel investor could also be
a good personal mentor for you.

A typical investment by angels could be anywhere
from $25,000 to $100,000. Often, if you go to a

group of angels, they will share the responsibility of due diligence, digging into all of your assumptions about and details of your business so that they gain comfort before investing their money.

Angel investing is a big market

Over $35 billion of angel investment was made in the U.S. alone last year, so we know that this is a robust field. Meeting these angels will require you to do some investigative reporting. Read some blogs, sign up for newsletters, look for angel groups in your city, and ask any VCs you meet at events about active angels in your area. Lawyers and accountants are also good sources for this information.

Venture Capitalists (VCs)

The third category of potential investors is venture capitalists or VCs. Unlike angel investors, VCs are not necessarily rich people, although many do happen to be rich. VCs have either strong financial or banking experience or strong operational experience, perhaps having been the CEOs of other startups. In a VC firm, such professionals come together as partners. Their job is to take money from large entities that have lots of money to invest, such as pension funds, university endowments, or trust funds with family wealth, and invest it in startups. They keep an eye on each new company's growth, then exit, returning most of the money back to their investors (keeping a sizable chunk for themselves).

Their goal is to make huge returns. Once they see an opportunity for their capital to help create a business of significant size and scale, they will invest millions of dollars into a startup. Then, they will work to create an "exit" for getting their investment back along with a sizable profit.

I will discuss this concept further in the next chapter of this book. In the meantime however, keep in mind how important the exit is to a VC. This exit usually means either the sale of the company (merger or acquisition) or an initial public offering (IPO) where shares of the company are floated on a stock exchange. It represents the only way a VC firm can get its money back.

These VC firms have their own criteria for deciding what kind of investments they will invest in. They take significant risks with the money they have raised, so they need to be careful about which companies they fund. Otherwise, they would find themselves losing the money that they raised from other people and large institutions.

The next chapter is devoted to VCs, and I have a lot more to tell you about them.

VC investments are risk capital.
(And that is good for you!)

Since it is risk capital, VC funding is unlike what a bank provides. Entrepreneurs seldom have any collateral to show when they seek funding. They need risk capital—funding from someone with deep pockets who can help with their growth and expansion—and they are willing to share their wealth with such an investor. VCs not only provide risk capital, they also provide guidance and valuable advice as well as connections. They have seen this movie before, and they can help entrepreneurs recognize trouble spots and provide preemptive guidance. Their value can be measured in more ways than just money.

Banks

The fourth category of investors is bankers. Banks are typically not the source of funding for entrepreneurs during the initial stages. This is because bankers, unlike VCs and angels, are sitting on the opposite side of the table from you. While VCs and angels make money only when you make money, banks work differently. They will only give you money if they can get some collateral from you. Even if you don't make money, they want to make sure that they get their capital back. A bank is not necessarily your friend, but once you start generating cash, or even when you get investments from some top-notch VCs, they will be more willing to offer you loans because you now have collateral.

Venture Debt

If you just raised $5 million from VCs, many bankers will be very interested in setting you up with what they call venture debt. Venture debt is a line of credit against the money you already have in the bank, the money that came from a VC. It may involve a promise from the VC stating that the VC firm will support your company and provide you with additional funding when necessary. This soft commitment from the VC firm becomes the bank's collateral. Of course, bankers also get additional stock in the company to compensate for this risk that they may be taking.

Bankers love to offer venture debts in which they provide you with a loan or a line of credit with a handsome interest and they take some warrants inside your company. Warrant coverage simply means that the bank gains some equity in your company. Equity can take the form of shares like the ones your VCs have received or will receive in the next round of funding. It may also take the form of an option to buy some shares in your company later at a predetermined price. Typically, banks hold 2% to 15% of warrant coverage, plus interest, as their equity stake in the company.

Warrants for venture debt

Here's an example of how warrants work: Say, your bank gives you $1 million in venture debt. This means that under certain conditions, you will be able to borrow up to $1 million from the bank without showing formal collateral. It will, of course, charge you interest on this money (the prevailing rate can be the prime rate plus 1%, which translates to something between 5% and 6% these days), plus a loan origination fee (assume another $10,000 to $25,000 to initiate this loan), plus 4% warrant coverage.

Warrants for venture debt
continued

What you get for this warrant coverage depends on what was negotiated. It can mean that the bank will get a right to buy $40,000 worth of shares at today's price anytime between now and the next ten years. (Note: 4% of a $1 million venture debt equals $40,000.)

If today's price is 40 cents per share, then over the next ten years, if the company does well, the bank can buy $40,000/$0.40, or 100,000 shares, for $40,000. If your share prices rise to $3 a share, the bank will get a handsome profit of $300,000. Thus, this warrant coverage balances the risk the bank takes by investing in a small, fledgling venture without collateral.

Venture debt can serve as a strategic tool for entrepreneurs. I myself have used it successfully at least twice. At one time, I was able to use venture debt to extend my runway by about six months. (Note: "runway" comes from the aviation term. Just as each airplane must have a certain length of runway for gaining speed and lifting off, your business must attain sufficient speed before its runway ends, or the results could be disastrous.) This allowed me to reach an important product development milestone and raise the next round of funding at a valuation of $16 million rather than $10 million. In another instance, I was able to bring the company to a stage where I could find it a suitable buyer. I was then able to pay off the venture debt line, once I closed down that round of funding. Ultimately, venture debt can be very valuable.

Venture debt can be tricky!

On the other hand, I have also lost a company due to venture debt. When things get tough, VCs and angel investors are generally willing and able to understand your difficult situation; they may even extend a rope. But bankers do not. As soon as they see things go bad, banks will step in and take their money. Many companies are lost due to venture debt.

My company Veridicom was in the business of making silicon fingerprint sensors like the ones you find in many laptops today. We had taken two patents from Bell Labs and raised $38 million in three rounds of funding to commercialize this technology. We had also secured a venture debt line of $6 million that we had used to extend our runway. When we got caught in the tech-bubble burst, our next round

of VC funding fell apart and, at the last moment, the
new VCs could not come through with the money.

We started working with our VCs to arrange alter-
nate funding, but the bank got nervous and invoked
the infamous MAC (Material Adverse Condition)
clause. This broad clause allows banks to terminate
your line of venture debt and call in the note (i.e.,
demand their money back) when they don't feel
"comfortable." When fear is in the air, they are not
afraid to invoke this clause. The result is disaster
for the startup company. When our bank called the
clause, the VCs gave up and asked us to hand over
the keys to the bank and go home.

(As a side note, the story is longer and it takes a
more positive turn. I was able to convince the bank
to let us sell our intellectual property and then return its money. The plan was unusual, but it succeeded. The bank got its money back over the next
six months, but I had to sell the company's assets
piece by piece in order to raise over $10 million
and pay back over $6 million in interest.)

Strategic Investors

The next category of investors is the strategic investor. Strategic investors are typically larger companies with a strategic interest in your technology or in the market segment in which you operate. Imagine that you are doing something innovative in the long-term care pharmacy market, a segment of the pharmacy field that involves delivering medication to seniors and other people living in special homes. These pharmacies are not open to retail customers; they supply medicine solely to nursing homes and specialty long-term care facilities.

Now, imagine a company that has a good retail pharmacy business. To them, you may represent a very interesting expansion niche. They see that you can make their business grow, so they might be interested in buying or acquiring your company. Possession of your company and its assets would allow them to enter into a market they're interested in without having to do all of the hard work that such an entrance generally requires. If you do all of the hard work for them, prove that there is a market for what you offer, and prove that revenue can be generated by it, then they might want to come in and buy your company.

Big companies want you!

Most corporate expansion happens through strategic acquisitions. You may seem interesting to another company because of the technology you are working on. Once it's proven to be valuable, they will want to have a close look at it, and they may even want to have the ability to acquire it.

Many large companies also have a strategic investment fund that they use for investing in startup companies. For an early-stage company, they will typically help out with one to two million dollars, with much larger amounts for later-stage companies. This sort of investment is very common in the pharmaceutical and drug market, but it also occurs in the software and hardware markets.

Pros and Cons of Seeking Strategic Investors
The good news about strategic investors is that they do more for you than simply provide funding. They can open doors for you to new markets and new customers through their sales channels. They can give you credibility, so that people take you more seriously. Usually, strategic investors are not that sensitive to the valuation of your company.

They don't worry about whether your company is valued at eight million, or ten million. They aren't that concerned, because their interest isn't in the valuation. It's in the technology.

The bad news is that by taking money from a strategic investor, you also shut yourself off from other business transactions. If there are two or three main players in one industry and you have investment from one of those companies, the rivals of that company may be suspicious of buying products from you. They may be unwilling to attempt to acquire you since they know that if they make an acquisition offer, a competitor who's already invested in you may have the right of first refusal. The "Right of First Refusal" clause gives an investor the right to review and match any acquisition offer that your company receives; only if he refuses to do so can you accept an acquisition offer from a third party. This is not an ideal clause from the entrepreneur's point of view since it limits one's options. Not only does it make a competing party reluctant to make an initial offer since its rival can always match it, but it also tips its hand by showing its strategic intentions.

This could end up tying your hands behind your back, so you need to ask yourself the following questions: Should I take this strategic money? When should I take it? Why should I take it? Nevertheless, taken with the right partner at the right time, strategic investments can be very valuable. Usually, however, the right time is in the later stage of your company, when you have revenue and you are looking to expand into new markets, or new countries.

CHAPTER 3

The Secret World of Venture Capitalists

V Cs, or venture capitalists, hold a special fascination for many entrepreneurs. Somehow, entrepreneurs look up to VCs as if they were kings or king-makers. In fact, VCs are simply finance people or entrepreneurs just like you who have succeeded in starting companies and creating wealth for their investors. VCs invest other people's money. They have to be out there raising new money, just like you may be trying to do as an entrepreneur. They raise money from institutional investors and fund-of-funds. Then, the venture funds (or VC firms) that the VCs work for carefully invest that money into individual startup companies, guiding them so that these startups can exit (by going public or being acquired) and then return the profits to the investors of these venture funds.

Glossary of terms

Fund-of-Funds: Professional companies that invest in VC funds rather than individual companies or ventures. These funds raise money from institutional investors and strategically sprinkle it among VC firms to diversify their risks with the intention of making money for their stakeholders.

Limited Partners (LPs): Institutions with large sums of money that must be invested in order to grow. (The State of Wisconsin Pension Fund is such an example. The billions of dollars contributed to it by state employees must be invested, and some of that money finds its way into high risk, high reward places known as venture capital.)

General Partners: The few main senior people of a company who come together to run a VC funds. Their job is to raise money for LPs and keep them happy. They invest LPs money in high potential startups, get them to exit, collect their returns, and send most of the money back to the LPs.

Large state, government, and corporate pension funds and endowments must invest and grow their money in order to meet their future financial obligations. They invest in stocks, real estate, currencies, and perhaps—a small amount—in venture capital assets.

Sometimes, very rich families and trusts establish relationships with VCs. They invest money into VC funds so that the VCs can be the professional managers of their risk capital. These institutions (pension funds, wealthy families, and trusts) become **limited partners (LPs)**_when they invest a portion of their assets with the venture capital firms (or VCs).

VC firms take money from these LPs and, over a period of seven to ten years, invest that money into startup companies. As each of their investments (the startups) exits, they return capital, hopefully with a large profit, back to the LPs. They accomplish this by providing startups with advice and board-level guidance to help them develop into large and profitable companies. The VCs realize these gains when their startup exits, either by going public (being listed on the stock market as an initial public offering, or IPO. This is sometimes referred to as "floating their shares on the market.") or by being acquired by yet another larger company.

VCs are not into "lifestyle businesses."

I want to make a point here about "lifestyle businesses." A lifestyle business is a business you can grow that, if it works, will be a cash cow for you over a long period of time. You often cannot, however, grow it to be a scalable and large enterprise within a short period of time, say, three to seven years.

Examples of such businesses may include grocery stores, restaurants, and other retail stores. These businesses are of no interest to VCs, but there are other types of investors, such as angel investors, that are more suitable for this type of business.

VCs only make their money once a company has a liquidity event—by being purchased by a bigger company or by going public—so shares can be sold in the open market. This is the only way they can recognize a gain on their initial investment. Each venture fund is bound by its bylaws to liquidate investments in a seven- to ten-year period and return the capital and profits back to its limited partners.

You may have a wonderful business that can keep on making cash for you, but if it will never scale, or you are not likely to have an exit, then you need to look elsewhere for your investor options.

Where Do VCs Get Their Money?

VCs get their money from their LPs, with whom
they have developed personal relationships. Fund
amounts vary from VC to VC. First-time VCs usually start with smaller funds as they still need to
prove to people that they are good money managers. More experienced VCs who have established
their credibility by showing prior success may deal
with much larger funds. While a typical fund is
usually between one hundred million and three
hundred million dollars, funds may contain as little as twenty or thirty million dollars or as much as
a billion dollars. Of course, there are always exceptions. There are seed funds that are as small as ten
million dollars, and large late-stage funds that are
two billion dollars.

The VC Model

The VC model works like this: A group of people
gets together and wants to raise money to start a
new VC fund. This is called raising a fund. Next,
they create an investment thesis, a premise on why
their fund can make money. For example, their investment thesis could point out that one of their
members has a unique background in a certain
technology area or has unique connections with

a certain university (e.g., many funds started in Cambridge, Massachusetts, claiming ties to MIT).

These "general partners" of the VC fund then meet with many "limited partners." They try to convince these LPs that their fund will make money for them. They may sell the fund idea based on its unique location (city or proximity to a university) or the backgrounds of the general partners, their track records, or some other angle. They want to convince the LPs that they can attract better entrepreneurs and make more money for them than other VCs can, all with less risk involved.

VCs also have to kiss a lot of frogs

It is not unusual for VCs to make dozens if not hundreds of their sales pitches to raise money. Hummer Winblad was such a venture fund. John Hummer was professional basketball player. His investment thesis was that most VCs invest within 10 to 20 miles of their offices, and no one pays attention to startups on the East Bay (the eastern side of San Francisco bay, including cities such as Oakland, Berkeley, and Walnut Creek).

VCs also have to kiss a lot of frogs
continued

Hummer raised his first VC fund money after making 124 unsuccessful pitches to LPs. But once he did manage to raise a venture fund, Hummer Winblad became very successful investing in software-only companies.

How Do VCs Make Money?

Once VCs raise a new venture fund, they make money in two ways: annual management fees and "carry." VCs take between 2% and 2.5% of the fund's value, every year, as their annual management fee (this is all negotiated with their LPs while they are raising funds); for example, a two hundred million dollar fund will have about four million dollars per year as a management fee. This amount is used to pay salaries, employee benefits, and travel and office expenses, as well as for other staff that need to be hired in a VC firm. That management fee gives VCs their day-to-day operational capital. Now you can see why more and more VC funds are getting bigger and raising bigger fund amounts. This is not good for entrepreneurs, as bigger funds must make bigger investments. As a result, this leaves out seed stage entrepreneurs.

The VCs' job is to find interesting companies that are capable of a great return. They then invest in these companies. They also usually come to sit on the boards of these companies and help guide them to an exit. The expectation is that, once a company is sold, the $10 million investment, for example, will become $150 million. If this occurs, the VCs will return the ten million dollars in original capital to their limited partners. Of the remaining $140 million, they will keep a portion for their own reward. This amount is called "carry." If the VC firm receives the typical carry of 20%, its reward in this example would be $28 million. The remaining profit is given back to the limited partners. You can see that their interests are aligned. VCs want to seek great returns. It helps them and it works for the LPs, which, in turn, allows VCs to raise subsequent funds.

The "carry" is typically 20 percent, but sometimes, for tier one funds that are very famous (since they have produced consistently superior returns for their LPs) and well established, it can be 25 to 35 percent. Limited partners are willing to pay this amount because these funds have a history of seeing great returns.

VCs and the gardener

The role of VCs is a little bit like that of gardeners: They have to plant a seed, nurture it, and make sure it grows. They need to be sure it receives the right amount of sunlight so that it grows into a strong tree, which can then be sold. Remember, not all gardeners have "green thumbs." You should look at their prior gardens before trusting them to plant your own. Yet, one must remember that the various conditions of nature can always impact a seed's ability to grow! The same implies for VCs. Some used to be good entrepreneurs themselves and, thus, understand the process of taking a company from being a mere idea to generating a profit. If your chemistry with them is good, they can be your mentors and you can learn from them. Others are hard to work with or add little value.

VCs are also quite interesting, because they have to find people to work for them who have one skill: they must be able to raise money through limited partners. Just as entrepreneurs must raise money from VCs, VCs must raise money from LPs. They have to be just as good as entrepreneurs at presenting their fund objective, their fund performance, their team members, and the kind of deal flow they can get. They need to convince LPs that they are worthy of their investment.

The nature of venture capital firms

It's important to understand one major difference between venture capital firms and other types of investors. VC firms are set up as investment funds. In this sense, they are like mutual funds, or hedge funds. They solicit money from investors (either individuals or institutions) and then take that money and use it to fund companies.

The point to keep in mind is this: The general partners in a VC firm have the same motivation as any fund manager—they want to make as much money as possible for their investors. When you keep this in mind, many of the actions and attitudes of VC firms start to make sense.

Limited Partners (LPs)

Limited partners are the source of money for VCs. The LPs can be large pension funds, university endowments, or any large family trust. They have large amounts of money, sometimes hundreds of billions of dollars, in their possession. The managers of this money need to find ways to make it grow in order for the LPs to be able to meet their obligations, such as a pension fund having to pay out its pensioners or, in the case of a university endowment, having to meet its operating expenses.

Examples of active limited partners for VCs

- State of Wisconsin pension fund
- California Public Employees' Retirement System, or CalPERS (Note: CalPERS has almost $180B of public money that must be invested)
- Harvard University Endowment
- Haas Family (founders of Levi Strauss Company)

Professional money managers work to make money for these institutions. They invest a certain percentage of the assets of the fund, endowment, or trust in the stock market, a certain percentage in the bond market, a certain percentage in real estate, and a certain percentage in currency hedges. They also take a small percentage of the money and invest it with VCs. The idea is that although the risk is higher, the reward may also be greater. If they get lucky, they can make up for all the risk they have taken and all the money they may have lost.

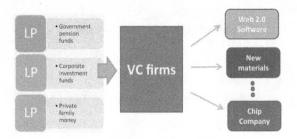

*Figure 1: How VCs raise money from Limited
Partners and Invest in many Startups*

It's also important to know that an LP only invests
with a VC for a definite period of time. LPs expect
to get their money back, and then some, within a
specific time frame.

It's not uncommon for LPs to each invest several
hundred million dollars in venture activity. They
will try to diversify their own risks by putting some
money in early-stage companies, some in VC funds
for mid-stage companies, and some in VC funds
that invest in late-stage companies. They may also
diversify by geography or sector. They may invest
in some VC funds that specialize in software companies and some that specialize in medical devices
or drug research. LPs use a variety of diversifica-
tion strategies in order to provide some protection
for their investments.

How VCs Invest the LPs' Money

When VC firms invest LPs' money, they try to diversify their risk by making investments in several different types of startups. For example, a VC fund can, based on the expertise of its general partners, be established with the charter to invest in Information Technology and Life Sciences. Within these broad areas of interest, it may then focus on "wireless infrastructure," or "drug discovery." These specific niche areas would be chosen based on the core expertise of the fund's general partners and the fund's "investment thesis." This thesis serves as the VCs' investment philosophy. It's the "story" that VCs told their LPs when they were raising money to establish this fund. It's often based on the VCs beliefs and their research on what segments of the market are most likely to do well in the coming years.

VCs may also invest in companies working in different aspects of the same industry. For example, when a VC fund invests in companies doing drug research, they put money in a company working on heart medicine as well as a company researching cholesterol medication. They diversify their own money so they will have stakes in different parts of the same market segment. In this way, they diversify their own risk. It is rare for VCs to invest in multiple companies in exactly the same area. How do you find out what areas a VC fund invests in? That is easy. Each VC fund tells you its main areas of investment on its website.

As an entrepreneur looking for funding, there are three things that you must remember to do when trying to decide which VCs to approach.

1) You should take a look at a VC's website to find out if your company matches their investment thesis. You will not be highly regarded as an entrepreneur if you pitch a clean tech deal to a VC who only invests in pharmaceutical and life science startups.

2) You should know what other companies have invested in and which partner is on which board. This way you know not to pitch to them if they have invested in your direct competitor.

3) If your needs are for seed-level capital, then you should not seek funding from a late-stage VC or a very large firm. They cannot be bothered with chasing small investments if they have raised a $1 bil-

lion fund. (See below to understand more about how VCs decide on where to invest.)

What vintage is your fund?

All VC funds are set up as partnerships with a finite life, and they will be dissolved after this time period is over. A typical VC fund has a life of ten years. When you approach VCs, you should know when their funds were formed. If a fund was formed seven years ago, then you know that it is almost at the end of the it's life and in two to three years the VCs will have to exit all of their investments, return profits to the LPs, and close out the partnership. This may not leave enough time for your company to be built right. The VCs will want to hurry you up. They will want to see a quick exit because they don't have the patience to sit another five to six years to see what kind of exit you will have.

It's like arriving at a restaurant just before closing time. Yeah, it's still open for business, and the cooks and waiters may still serve you, but they may also try to get you to hurry up and finish your meal by closing time because they want to go home. The same principle applies to the life of a VC fund. You want to approach a fund that is still fresh and early in its life so that you will have more time to build the company that you want to build and not be rushed to have an exit before you have reached your full potential as a company.

Discover a VC Fund's Focus

After learning the vintage of the VC fund, the next thing an entrepreneur needs to do is learn what kind of companies the VCs have invested in. If they have already invested in the sector you are in, they are unlikely to invest in that sector again. Your meeting with them will be for their benefit, so they can learn something about the market from your perspective. They won't necessarily be looking to fund you. However, if a VC has been looking to fund in a certain area but hasn't found the right company yet, then you have a higher probability of connecting with him. Do some homework before you approach a VC fund. Is it really looking to invest in your sector, or is it just fishing for information?

The definition of a sector must be carefully understood. Wireless is a sector, but it is huge. You can be investing in wireless infrastructure, wireless contents, wireless advertising, or wireless devices. These are all very different subsectors, and a VC firm can have investment in each of these (and many other) subsectors. This should not discourage you. If the firm has invested in a mobile advertising company, then it is unlikely that it will invest in a second mobile advertising company. It would rather diversify its positions by going to an adjacent sub-sector.

You can find out what companies these VCs have invested in by simply searching the Internet. Look at the VC firm's website, and also look at the companies that service this industry.

Helpful links

The website of the National VC Association is http://nvca.org/.

A great resource for finding the top VC firms is http://www.entrepreneur.com/vc100 is.

Go to http://www.theFunded.com to get all the dirt on VC firms from entrepreneurs. Both VC firms and individual VCs are rated here. These are user-generated opinions, so take these with a grain of salt.

The Anatomy of a VC Firm

The third thing that is important for an entrepreneur to do is to understand the anatomy of a VC firm. A venture capital firm can have anywhere from two to ten partners, but five or six is a typical number. It is a partnership and, thus, has its own dynamics since it is typically not hierarchical. Each partner will be a specialist in some area. Each specialty is in a certain type of company or industry, based on the partner's experience. All partners are expected to go out and find deals worth investing in.

How Many Companies Does a Fund Invest In?

How many deals a VC fund invests in depends on how much money it has raised and how many partners it has. A common scenario is this: a mid-stage fund sets aside fifteen to twenty million dollars for each investment it plans to make even though the initial investment may only be five million dollars. If the company is successful, the VC fund will want to have enough of what they call "dry powder." This is the VC term for cash available for future rounds of funding in a company. VC funds want to be able to invest additional funds and participate in future investment rounds in order to maintain their portion of ownership of the company.

From the VC perspective, one of the worst things that can happen is to have money put in a company, have that company become quite successful, and then not have any money available to participate in subsequent funding. The VC firm's percentage of ownership will shrink, and it will most likely feel that it deserves a bigger return (by keeping a bigger share of the company) after having taken such a great risk during early-stage investment. The VC will have done all the necessary hard work, and the company will start becoming successful, but the VC won't be able to fully participate in the success. To keep this from happening, the VC will typically set aside two to three times the amount of the initial investment for future investment. If the initial investment is five million dollars, he may set aside another ten million for the future.

For seed stage funds, the concept is the same but the amount will be smaller. A fund may only invest five hundred thousand or one million dollars but set aside three to five million dollars for use in future investment rounds in case the company is successful.

This information helps you analyze a VC fund in the following way: If there is a $300M[1] fund and you know from looking at its website that it has four partners, then you can presume that each partner

_____

1   M stands for million

will look after about one quarter of the fund amount. Since any single partner is not likely to be sitting on more than four or five boards, you can also assume that around $15M is set aside per company. Yes, for each investment that a VC firm makes, one partner assumes at least one board seat in order to keep an eye on the company invested in and guide it. Doing the arithmetic, you can conclude that VCs will be able to do twenty investments during the life of this fund and they are likely to put $3M to $5M into the initial investment so they will have another $10M or more reserved for follow-up investments. You will also recognize that they need to put the invest-ment money to work in the first three to five years of the fund's existence, or it will be too late. The fund's life will be coming to an end by the time a company matures and gets ready for an exit since it typically takes a company five to seven years to do so. Of course, there are exceptions to this rule, and some companies grow very fast and have quick exits, but VCs generally don't plan to be so lucky.

Why are VCs so tough to please?

Some entrepreneurs believe that VCs are just evil. They believe that VCs are there to rip their plans to shreds and kill their dreams. The reality, of course, is that the vast majority of VCs are hard-working people who are trying to make money for their investors: the Limited Partners.

VCs have to be tough for a couple of reasons. For one thing, as you will see in the next section, they get more funding requests than they could ever possibly serve. They have to make some hard decisions when it comes to deciding which companies to invest in. It is supply and demand. A typical Silicon Valley VC fund gets between two and five thousand business plans or requests per year, but it is likely to make only three to five investments per year. The odds are tough that it will be you! You really have to be exceptional and stand out.

The second reason is that although they want the companies they invest in to succeed, their primary loyalty lies with the investors whose money they are managing. This means they need to give a rigorous examination to any startup that they consider. They owe it to their investors to make sure the companies they fund have the potential to reap big returns during the life of the VC fund.

What are Your Odds of Being Funded by a VC?

Most VC funds will receive several thousand business plans per year to look at. Each partner may receive between one and two thousand business plans. Many of these plans come in unsolicited, but many of them come through referrals. The referrals might come from colleagues, other people the VCs know in the industry, university professors, or business partners. From the one to two thousand business plans they receive, however, each VC may carefully look at only one to two hundred. That's only ten percent of the total received.

From those one to two hundred reviewed plans, the VC will probably take a close look at no more than twenty of them, investigating their potential through meetings with company leaders. From those twenty, maybe three or four will actually make it to the final stages of the process and will actually put out a term sheet and an invitation to invest. The bottom line is that from the thousands of business plans received, each partner of a fund will probably invest in one or two companies per year. If a partner invests in one or two companies per year, in about three years, he or she will have five to seven companies that each VC partner can invest in. If every partner holds the maximum number of board positions that he or she can manage, the fund will have as many investments as it can handle during its existence.

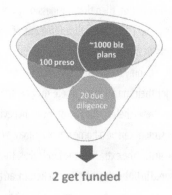

2 get funded

Just look at the odds. Even after you have done your homework and sent in your plan and even though you had a referral, you still have a one-in-a-thousand chance of getting funded by a VC! You have to work extremely hard in order to have even a chance with them. Getting money from a VC is not easy. That is why you have to be very prepared. Your business plan has to be solid, and you must have customer traction and an excellent team in place. You will need all the help you can get to be ready for that level of engagement.

Big returns for VCs?

How big are the returns a VC gets for his or her investments? VCs aim for the possibility of making five to ten times the amount invested. If a VC cannot see a way to making a 10X return, then that business may not fit into the fund's criteria. VCs know that three out of every ten investments that they make will die and four to six will be mediocre or only moderately successful—they will be lucky to get their money back. There may be one or two home runs. Nevertheless, they must invest believing that every investment can be a home run or a runaway success in order to justify the extra risks the fund takes. The returns are measured in IRR, or Internal Rate of Return, an annualized rate of money invested and returns received.

The Profile of a VC

Many VCs are either people who came out of investment banking and really understand money, or they are experts in running a certain type of company. Normally, if you are a successful founder of or an executive in a company that a fund has invested in <u>and you made money for the fund by creating a successful exit</u>, you may be <u>invited</u> to join the firm. Yes, this is a by-invitation-only type of a job.

It's almost impossible to simply apply and get hired inside a firm, as it is very much a close-knit group. If you have to ask to be hired, you will probably be rejected. You will not be invited without a good track record. The only exception is this: VC firms do tend to take some top-notch students from the best business schools. If you are a Harvard or Stanford business school graduate, then you may have a chance to come in as an associate and work your way up in the organization.

Inside Structure of a VC Firm

The VC firm looks like this: There are general partners, usually in their late 30s to their late 50s, who have the operational experience. They have worked with many companies, and they really know about the venture business. They know how to grow a business. Then there will sometimes be principals and associates. These people are on their way to becoming future general partners, but they still need to learn more about the method and the process. Often they are the ones who do a lot of heavy lifting. They perform with due diligence, investigating market segments and identifying promising startups and entrepreneurs. Then there are interns, and of course, the secretarial support staff. You will also sometimes see people known as "EIR." That can either stand either for "Entrepreneur-In-Residence" or, based on the firm's culture, "Executive-in-Residence." I will explain the role and purpose of an EIR below.

How you are likely to be treated by a VC

I don't want you to freak out, but often first-time entrepreneurs have a negative impression of VCs after their first meeting. I have heard tons of stories about how a VC was late to the meeting, he did not really pay attention, he was looking at his Blackberry the whole time the entrepreneur was presenting, and he did not really understand the idea being presented. Then he unceremoniously took a pass on investing in the company. While some of these stories are justified, many are not. It has to do with seeing things from their lens.

Most entrepreneurs come in not knowing how to present their business plans effectively. Most entrepreneurs don't know how a VC wants to consume the data that they plan to throw at them. Don't expect the VCs to have read your material in advance. They are not so interested in your technology or the dozens of slides about technology and patents, yet. Once you hook them, then you will find them truly interested and paying a lot more attention.

How you are likely to be treated by a VC
continued

First of all, they must believe in the market where your business will operate and its market dynamics. If they agree with your data and your command of the market, then they need to see you and your team as investment-worthy. Only after these two tests are passed will they want to learn about the intricacies of your technology.

They may not be polite enough to let you go through your presentation without questioning you. They need to absorb the data in the order that makes sense to them. They may look bored or disinterested, but they may not be. You will be surprised at their ability to spot holes and dive in for more details in areas that matter to them.

This is why it is of utmost importance to leave at least 15 minutes before the hour is over for Q&A. You must limit your presentation to 20 minutes or so during a one-hour meeting so that they can explore, ask questions, and be intrigued.

Remember you are not trying to "close the deal" on the first meeting. Your only purpose is to get a second meeting.

EIR Programs

Many VC firms will invite <u>proven</u> entrepreneurs to come work in their offices in hopes that they will start a wonderful company soon. In some cases, the firm will even pay these EIRs reasonable salary so they don't have to worry about making a living. Someone who is invited to be an EIR (Entrepreneur-in-Residence) can get paid for six to twelve months. In that time, if he or she is able to take an idea and develop it into a company that can be funded, the firm will want the first dibs on funding it.

Of course, the firm will only do this with people they trust, smart people they have some history with. Chances are, smart people will start good companies, and the firm will want to be first in line to invest in them.

Sometimes, these positions will be known as "Executives-in–Residence," and could include any good talent, such as a VP of marketing or maybe a CEO candidate who just became available after one of the VC fund's portfolio companies was acquired. The VC firm wants to lock this "proven" executive in to use in one of its other portfolio companies. The

VC firm uses this technique to lock in talent. It's all about talent.

How VCs Evaluate a Company

When VCs look at a company, they are looking at answering three main questions:

1) Is this a large and growing market where we can make money?

2) Is this the team who has the potential to make us money? Can they execute and work together?

3) Is there enough money to be made in order to make it worth our time and effort (based on your business model, unique sustainable positioning, and financial assumptions)?

When they listen to your pitch, they are trying to sort out these three questions. If they are sufficiently intrigued, you will be asked to come back again, and you will get a chance to present your other 65 slides that you had in your back-up slide deck. Please try not to present they whole story in your first meeting. Tell them just enough for them to be intrigued. Leave them wanting more!

Syndication

There is another odd thing about VCs. When they see a good company, they seldom want to go in alone. They almost always want to bring in one or, sometimes, two other firms with them. It is partly quid pro quo, so that other firms will invite them to join in on a good deal. But it is also a way for them to de-risk the deal and benefit from the experience and wisdom of another firm's partner, who will sit next to them on the board. This is called syndication. You may be working with several VCs all at the same time, hoping to get them all to invest. This is not likely to happen. If one of them is interested, they will bring other VCs and create their own syndicate. They are very particular about whom they sit next to.

Multiple funds within a VC firm

An established VC firm usually starts raising a new fund after half of the first fund is invested. It can take one to two years to raise a new fund (unless you are a hot top-tier VC, and then it can be done much faster). Sequoia Capital is on its 12th fund. This means they have multiple funds that are at various stages of their lives. A fund typically has a seven- to ten-year life in which it makes investments and then seeks exits for its portfolio companies.

Multiple funds within a VC firm
continued

If a firm raised a fund in 1999, it may try to raise another fund in 2002 or 2003 (depending on how the first fund was panning out and if they had a compelling investment thesis). Then perhaps they will raise another fund in 2007. Each of these funds can have the same focus, or one fund may be raised to explore a specific type of investments or a particular region. We have seen some firms raise a new fund just to invest in clean energy or biotechnology.

Some companies have raised funds just to invest in India, for example. Kleiner Perkins raised a $100 million fund that only invests in iPhone applications development. It is not uncommon for successful VC firms to have several funds active at any given time.

What to Expect from a VC

VCs expect you, the entrepreneur, to run the company. Do not expect them to run your company or make decisions for you. They are too busy to be able to spend a lot of time on any one company. They will invest in you. If a VC is spending a lot more time with you, it's usually a bad sign. It means that they no longer trust you to run the company well.

VCs will show up for a monthly board meeting. There is no way that they can know more about what you do day to day than you and your team knows. There is a whole art to managing your board that I discuss in a separate e-book. But I will spend some time on this topic in Chapter 11 of this book as well.

You can request and count on the VCs who serve as your board members (you will also have some board members who are not VCs) to do the following:

1) Be available for occasional strategy consultation;

2) Attend your board meetings, and be available perhaps once in between the meetings;

3) Be willing to make introductions to other VCs or strategic partners or customers if they have a good personal relationship with other parties;

4) Be willing to interview your key senior executive team members during the hiring process.

As you can see above, these are high-level strategic actions. VCs should not—and will not–make day-to-day decisions for you. They won't even help you land a major contract of any sort, unless there are strategic reasons why their presence will help them or your company in a major way.

Most first-time entrepreneurs have much higher expectations from their VCs. They soon find out that they will need to do their own heavy lifting.

There is a lot more to be discussed about VCs, how to approach them, and how to raise money from them. All of this will be discussed in the chapters that follow. In this chapter I wanted you to have a better sense of who these VCs are, what drives them, and what their principal role is. This background knowledge will be very helpful if you end up approaching them for investing in your startup.

Catching a VC's attention

VCs see hundreds of deals a year. Last year one firm told me that they saw 4,500 deals last year alone. So you can just imagine how quickly you have to move to find the gem among them. If something catches their attention, they capture it. If it doesn't, they move on immediately and you will know it. Sometimes, during the presentation, you'll see them checking their Blackberries; that means that you have already lost their attention. And that's not a good sign.

You have to be able to get your point across to them. Don't try to fill every square inch of the paper with text and ink and try to conquer the world. You have to be very direct and very succinct and very quickly get their attention. If you don't maintain their attention during the first three minutes of the presentation, I suspect it will be very hard to regain it.

CHAPTER 4

Investors' Motivations and Your Funding Strategy

As we have seen, investors come in various shapes and sizes. Each can be useful for entrepreneurs at different stages of their lives. But another question needs to be asked: What is the investor's Return on Investment (ROI) and what are they seeking?

Why Angel Investors Invest

When angel investors invest, they are looking to increase their wealth, but often that is a secondary objective. Their primary objective is usually to spend time with smart, interesting people or in market segments that are interesting to them. (Since they are already rich, presumably they don't *need* to make more money.) It's a way for them to stay engaged and stay fresh. Of course, they want a high return, but it's not the only thing that drives them. They are less sensitive than most VCs.

Why VCs Invest

VCs are professional money managers, so they are solely interested in the investment return for their limited partners. They will squeeze you on the valuation of your company. They will also stay quite involved on the board level. They want to make sure that you do things right and your motivations are correct. Often, entrepreneurs get worried and begin to assume that VCs are trying to screw them over or that they are not acting in the company's best interest.

Keep in mind that a VC has only one objective: to make a high return for their limited partners. You may have multiple objectives. Your ego may be in play, you may have a desire to hang on to a title, or you may want to build a company to show off to your friends and family that you did it. But for VCs, the only motivation is to make money. Of course, you will occasionally come across a bad apple, but in general, all a VC wants is a high return. You need to understand their motivation.

This is also why many entrepreneurs worry about keeping 51% control of their companies. Really, that is not important. Ownership does not guarantee control. Most of the control of the company comes from the board and what the bylaws of the company say, and when VCs invest their money, they will make sure that the board is either neutral or in their control even if they own less than 51% of your company.

Control vs. Ownership

Here is a typical example of how control of the company is exerted at the board level: Say the VCs hold two board seats, the CEO or founder holds one or two seats, and a fifth "independent" person is on the board. The VCs may select this fifth person, or you can negotiate a mutually agreed-on choice. In either case, there will be a board that is neutral, or maybe slightly favorable towards the VCs. This is where most of the decisions are made. Investors almost always get "preferred shares" when they invest money. This class of shares has special rights that are granted to the investors since they are putting in real cash. These rights are meant to protect their investments, and these special rights are the real instruments of control. Most company decisions are never brought out for a shareholder vote (the company bylaws or State and Federal regulations dictate this) and are instead made by the Board of Directors of the company. So, even if you hold 51% of the shares, you may never get to vote. Typically, the topics that require a shareholder vote include the issuing of additional shares or the sale of the company.

The bottom line is that once you take money from investors who really have to align your interests with theirs, they will have control over your company. You can only hope that your execution and vision are well aligned with theirs.

Don't confuse control with ownership

Control is exerted by professional investors in multiple ways. Stock ownership is only one of those ways. You may see keeping 51% control as a huge issue, but in fact it is only a part of the overall picture. The control on most decisions comes from board majority and rights that you find in the stock purchase agreement that you sign when you sell equity in your company, such as veto rights, information rights, and liquidation preferences. I will be explaining these terms later in the book.

Don't confuse control with ownership
continued

Often, only two kinds of decisions come to a shareholder vote: decisions to sell the company shares or to issue more shares. Even if an entrepreneur has a 51% majority in stock ownership, the only two times he or she would get to vote would be when the company is trying to increase the number of shares or when there is a change of control of the company (like a merger). Most decisions never come to a shareholder vote. Control of the company is exerted at the Board of Directors level. VCs will make sure that their money is not given to people (read "you") who still control the "steering wheel."

VCs' Investment Criteria

VCs usually have a goal to make five to ten times the money they invest in a company. If they cannot see a way to make five or ten times their investment in the five to seven years before the exit must happen, then their interest level will go down. No matter what projections you come up with, they will do their own computation based on their own internal analysis.

Your "Big Idea" is not the most important criteria

You may be surprised to know that your "brilliant idea" is not what attracts VCs to you. Their criteria include first and foremost the targeted market. Is this a large or growing market? If it is a large enough market and your company can get a small piece of it, VCs will be golden. A brilliant idea in a small market can still result in a small outcome for them. This does not mean that it is not a great company for the entrepreneur to start, but it is not a great company for the VC to invest in.

The second most important criterion is the team. Who is on the team? Youthful energy or seasoned and experienced entrepreneurs? Who has the team been able to attract as their advisors or board members? If the idea has attracted luminaries in that field, it says a lot about how good the idea is or any future morphed version of it can be.

The actual idea is the next most important criterion. A really cool idea that fits an unmet need is a good start, but the VCs know from having been in the business that the idea is likely to change—perhaps significantly—over time. This is why it is the third most important factor they consider.

VCs know that even after all their careful analyses, it is only one or two companies out of ten that will be a real success and return large sums of money (if they are lucky! There is much uncertainty that surrounds any investment that they make). Two or three companies will die completely, and five or six will just be zombies, walking-dead companies that are not bad enough to die but not going anywhere fast. But for VCs to take a chance with your company, they need to have at least a probability of high return. Their interests are purely financial.

VC Firm Size and Tiers

VC firms come in all sizes and shapes. It is important to study these firms as each has its own method and style of investing and nurturing its investments. Will their styles match yours? Try to meet people who have received investment from them and explore what it would be like to work with these investors.

Large firms—like Sequoia Capital, which has invested in Google and YouTube—will not want to invest in any company unless they can determine that their investment will result in a return of $100M^2$ or more. Their thesis is that the amount of time their partners invest in a company is the same, whether the company is sold for $100M (their portion may be $20M to $30M) or $500M. So, why not go after the big fish in the sea, i.e., startups that have the potential to scale and became significant companies and have very big exits? This thesis also dictates their typical desire to own 25% or more of your company no matter what the initial investment size may be. (This holds true for every VC firm when there is more than one participating in a round of funding.)

Smaller firms may be more flexible with their investment thesis and can spend more time with you. An example would be ATA Ventures or Labrador Ventures. These firms may have fewer partners, although the partners are no less accomplished than those at a larger firm. They are more willing to nurture companies and offer better valuations to attract good entrepreneurs. (Valuation is what your company is estimated to be worth by an investor. This amount dictates at what share price the investor will purchase shares in your company.)

---

2   M in this book indicates "million."

Doing your homework here does pay off.

Levels of VC firms

As in any other industry, there is a pecking order of VC firms. Some are more successful, while others are less so. According to entrepreneur Paul Graham, VC firms tend to perpetuate their levels of success. Firms that find success tend to be able to pick from the best startups, while lower-level firms fund less attractive startups.

While everyone wants to work with a top-level VC, there can be advantages to working with a mid-level VC firm. One advantage is that it may give you a more favorable valuation of your company, meaning they take less of a piece of it. A second advantage is that you will likely be able to negotiate better terms so that you retain greater control over your company.

Of course, lesser-regarded VC firms don't have the connections and mentoring capabilities that better firms have. But don't disregard lower-level VC firms. You might become their first big success story!

Why Do Strategic Investors Invest?

The strategic investor's criterion is primarily focused on the future. Of course, strategic investors *are* interested in making financial returns, but they are more interested in your technology, your team, or the market segment you are trying to work in. They compute their returns slightly differently from VCs. Often, they will invest in a company just to have board observer rights. That way they have some idea what the company is doing. They want to know about the technology and new markets that you may enter, but they have little interest in getting a financial return from you.

It's important for you to figure out what motivates the particular investors you are dealing with at the moment. Once you understand what drives them, you can figure out ways to make your pitch interesting to them.

Your Investment Strategy

It is important, now that you have a better idea of who the likely investors for your venture are, to come up with an investor strategy. It will largely depend on your specific needs, but in general, you should do the following:

1) Plan to bootstrap while you validate your main assumption and develop a business plan.

2) Start recruiting team members right away. This includes co-founders, professionals such as lawyers and advisors, and advisory board members. Also start identifying potential customers.

3) Make a list of angel-type investors. Identify their names, organizations, affiliations, and possible connections so you can figure out ways to reach them.

4) Research VC firms' websites to pick out which would be ideal and which would be a good second choice.

5) Research the partners that you think will be best suited to hear your pitch and put together a list of your connections that may be able to introduce you to them.

Once you have these lists, it will be a lot easier to make the connection when you meet people at networking events. You will also know what to do when you come across others who may be willing to connect you, mentor you, or invest in you.

Now you are ready to move to the next section! We will take a closer look at you as an entrepreneur and whether you are really ready to seek investment.

Prepare Yourself for Seeking Funding

In the last section, we examined the type of investors that you are likely to see, the methods they use to identify investment-worthy companies, and their motivations for investing. Now, we turn our attention to the startup that is seeking funding. In this section, we will cover you, the entrepreneur. You have to be ready before you approach these investors, and I set the bar high by making sure that you are "bullet proof."

Most entrepreneurs approach investors ill prepared. The typical thinking is, "Now that I have an idea, I must seek funding. After that, I will make a prototype and hire somebody to start selling." Nothing could be further from the truth. The right sequence is this:

1) I have an idea, let me validate it.
2) I will conduct market research to better understand my customers, their needs, and the way they go about purchasing products and services.
3) I will then find a customer and get him/her excited about my solution.
4) I will bootstrap until I get traction with my market and customers.

5) Once I have traction, I will approach investors to raise money.

6) Somewhere along the way, I will set up a legal entity and recruit a team of equally devoted, passionate, world-class people.

This sounds hard. But in fact, this is exactly what most startup companies do. This is the method and mindset that you should adopt.

CHAPTER 5

How to Get Investor-Ready: A Must-Do Checklist

The best way to get to a VC, or any investor, is to be properly introduced to them by a person they trust. Investors get thousands of requests per year. Entrepreneurs often throw their business plans at them in hopes of getting funded. This method seldom works. But if you are introduced through a referral from a professor, an advisor, an entrepreneur they have funded before, a law-firm partner, or someone else they have a relationship with, then you have a much better chance of getting an audience.

Even these intermediaries can be choosy. They know they get only a limited number of chances to show investors something interesting. If they show their investor colleagues three or four companies that are not quite ready for prime time, chances are these investors won't take their next phone calls, so they must be very choosy about the companies they bring to their VC friends. They must know a VC's thought process and criteria.

In my book *Seven Steps to a Successful Startup*, I discuss the minimum steps you need to take in order to be VC-ready. But just to summarize here, this is the list of questions to determine whether you are investor ready:

1) Do you have some market validation data? Is there really an unmet need?

2) Do you have any market traction? A proof point?

3) Do you have clarity on who your customers are and how many of them are out there (how big your market is)?

4) What is your comparative landscape? Who else is out there trying to solve the same problem that you intend to solve? How is their positioning different from yours? Where are they trying to go? How will you be successful vis-à-vis other competitors?

5) How will you make money (what is your business model)?

6) What are your financial assumptions?

7) What are your financial projections for the next five years? Revenue and profit? What are the key performance indicators that you will be watching as you grow your business?

8) Do you have a team that has a history of working together and a history of being successful?

Those are the eight checkpoints that VCs are going to look at. If you don't score high on these points, or you don't have a very compelling explanation as to why you don't score high, you are not VC ready. In fact, the same eight items are applicable to all investor types. The only difference with VCs is that all points have to be even more solid, because they won't give you as much leeway.

When you approach an angel, you may have a reasonable handle on the first four points, but five, six, and seven may be works in progress, and they will accept that. They will work with you. When you go to friends and families, you may only have number one or two, or maybe just one—market validation—confirmed. That may be good enough for them.

Don't approach investors too soon!

You only have one or two chances with an investor, so you really should be ready with all of the facts before you go see them. You will be judged on several things before you get to present your idea.

Investors invest in entrepreneurs who demonstrate a profound understanding of the dynamics of their markets and demonstrate "intense customer knowledge." Notice that I did not say anything about your technology or your solution. As I mentioned in the last section, it is about the market first, and then it is about the team. Investors know that your idea will morph as you spend more time understanding the dynamics of your market and getting close to your customers. And a good team in a large and growing market is likely to hit upon something good soon enough.

Be really prepared with data based on market research. The two things that take the longest as you prepare for investors are: 1) doing market research and 2) creating a financial model so that you can predict what will happen given some starting assumptions.

> ### Don't approach investors too soon!
> ### *continued*
>
> Entrepreneurs who try to short-circuit these two issues can run into significant headwinds. It is true that some companies have gotten started with just a proper financial spreadsheet (e.g., Facebook, Twitter, and YouTube), but investors knew that if these companies worked there would be a huge opportunity to monetize. They bet on the team and the market—and in these cases, it paid off. But, please don't plan on being lucky. You may get lucky, but you can't bet your future on it.

So, these are the eight points you should be using to evaluate your company before you approach investors. Now, allow me to give you a little bit more detail about what I mean regarding these items.

Market Validation and the Unmet Need

How do you know there is an unmet need? How have you proven that there really is a demand for the solution you are trying to provide? Most entrepreneurs make the mistake of starting out by talking about their technology or product. This is not the right place to start. What you need to do is show that there is an unmet need.

There are many ways to prove that there is an unmet need. You can conduct online surveys, meet face-to-face with people, conduct group discussions, or collect published information from newspapers and the internet. I talk about all these methods of determining whether there is a need for your product (and many more) in my e-book on market research, *Market Research on a Shoestring: Get a Reality Check on Your Big Idea for Under $100*. It's available at www.fivemountainpress.com. After reading that book, you will know how to demonstrate that there is a market for your product.

Market Traction Proof Point

Even if you have market validation, you need to know that people will buy your solution at your price. That is traction. The best way to show traction is by getting purchase orders from true customers. Being able to collect cash helps establish your case. You know there is traction at that point because people are paying you with hard cash to buy your solution. Think of traction as a pyramid (see diagram below). Actual sales are at the top of the pyramid. That is proof that there is a market for your product or service.

But sometimes it is not possible to get to revenue before you have to seek funding. Certain hardware products require a lot of money before even a prototype can be created. In this case, you want to go down the pyramid of traction shown below.

The higher you are on the pyramid of traction, the more fundable you become.

If you don't have actual sales (proof of traction), then the next level is customers using your product on a trial basis or as a pilot project. Perhaps you have made an agreement that they will pay you once they feel satisfied (conditional purchase order). That shows some traction. If you don't have that, the next level of the pyramid could be that you have people who have agreed to buy or to do a trial at a certain price, once you have the product.

If you don't even have that, then the next level of traction is to have people that you have spoken to who have said that your product is the kind of thing they are looking for, and that they are willing to buy it at a certain price. Ideally these potential customers (prospects, as we call them) have heard your pitch and can be used as references. If investors call them, they will give you a positive reference. If you don't have that, the next level of traction (towards the bottom of the pyramid) would be people you have spoken with who, although they are not saying they are willing to buy your product, say that it is a good idea. They agree that there is a problem that needs to be solved.

If you don't have that, the bottom of the pyramid is that you have lists of people you plan to talk to and discuss your idea. You're going to see if they might be interested in your product. If you don't even have names of people who might be interested, then you have zero traction. The higher up you are on this traction pyramid, the more convincing you will be to investors. VCs will want to talk to these customers and prospects before they make their decision. If you don't even know who your initial customers will be, then you have no game!

Target Customers and Market Size

You need to be ready with market-size data. My e-book on market research provides you with details on how to get this data. The more you know about who your customers are and how many of these customers are out there, the more convincing you will be.

VCs are interested in large and/or growing markets. A market size of $1 billion and above is very attractive. There is nothing wrong with small markets (such as $100 million a year), but you as an entrepreneur must be right in most of your decisions in order to hit a sizable chunk of a small market. Even then, the rewards for investors would be small. If your company is sold for $50 million after five years, that might be a reasonable exit return if you have 10% of the company. But for a VC to see her $4 million investment return only $10 million after five years of hard work may not be attractive. Smaller VC funds or angel investors may find this acceptable, but large VC firms will not be attracted to smaller exits.

Competitive Landscape

You need to have a profound understanding of the dynamics of your market. Entrepreneurs who demonstrate that kind of in-depth knowledge know all their competitors, their strategies, their projected trajectories, and how all these things provide opportunities. You should be able to demonstrate that your competitors are focused on a different market, or a different segment of your market, or that they have a different business model. You should be able to prove that you can succeed because your model is different or because you are taking a different approach. This would be compelling.

You must also be able to clearly communicate who else is meeting your customers' needs, and how you can do so more easily, more profitably, or faster than they can. What is your positioning? Do you understand where your competitors are heading? Do you know where are they likely to be when you enter the market? It is most important for an investor to know that you know this information. There is nothing more devastating than an investor listening to your pitch and then going back and discovering names of competitors that you did not bring up in your presentation simply by Googling and searching on the Internet.

Business Model

Your business model is how you plan to make money. It answers the questions "who will pay you?" and "whom do you have to pay?". Each business makes money in some unique way. Based on your customer interactions and market study, you should have some clarity on this topic. You must make a convincing case about the way you plan to make money.

Your business model should include your price, your customer acquisition cost, your per transaction profit (gross profits), and your ability and plans to scale this model.

Financial Assumptions

The next topic is financial assumptions. Each business should have two, three, or four main financial assumptions. You need to understand what they are and why you have arrived at these assumptions. You need to be completely clear about them.

The Restaurant Example

For example, if you want to get into the restaurant business, you might use three main financial assumptions. The first is how much money each table will spend. (Let's say your assumption is that each table will spend $42 dollars.) Your second assumption is how many times in one night a table will turn over. (You come to believe that one table can be turned over three times per night. This means each table will yield $42 for the five o'clock seating, plus another $42 for the seven o'clock seating, and another $42 for the nine o'clock seating.) Your third assumption is regarding what percentage of the tables are occupied in any given week. (Suppose your assumption is that seventy percent of the tables will be occupied on average.)

Building upon your assumptions

Now you can build a financial projection built on these three financial assumptions. You will set up your business and watch to see if these assumptions are true. Let's say you find out that each table is averaging $26 per seating. Now, you need to do something to get customers to spend $42. Maybe you will add some new menu items or encourage people to order an item from a new 'Appetizers' page. Perhaps, you will add new liquors or drinks to the wine menu. Or, you can change the décor of your joint so people think of it as a higher-class restaurant. Then, you can increase your prices.

Sensitivity Analysis and "What if" Scenarios

Using the same restaurant and assumptions, what if you discover that tables are turning an average of two times per night, not three times as predicted? You may want to change the music so that faster songs are played, or you may hire speedier waiters who will make sure that dinners are finished in two hours so new people can sit down.

These are examples of the kinds of assumptions that can drive your projections. You need to know what your assumptions are and how you will monitor them. A good investor will expect you to be able to clearly explain your ideas about assumptions. You will also need to show how you arrived at these assumptions.

Key Performance Indicators (KPIs) and Financial Projections

Based on the assumptions you've made, you should be able to build projections concerning the sales you will have year one, year two, etc., up to year five. This can be longer for bio tech companies, since it takes longer than that for them to show significant progress or traction. The same is true for company expenses, in those first years, and projected profits.[3] You really need to be able to understand key performance indicators for your industry. They determine how you gauge the progress of the company and what projections for revenue, profits, and growth are reasonable. .

In my restaurant example, it may be that you looked at the menus of every restaurant in the area where you are planning to start your business, and you figured out the average amount spent by the clientele of restaurants similar to yours. You may also visit comparable restaurants in other parts of town and try to talk to waiters on their breaks, while they are smoking a cigarette in the alley. Ask questions and calculate the typical spending per table. When you want to validate how many times per night a table turns over, you may sneak a look in the window at a few restaurants for a few nights and take some data yourself. That will tell you what the typical turnover rate is.

---

3   I have described in great detail how to create such projections in my e-book *Finance Essentials for Entrepreneurs*, which is also available at www.five-mountainpress.com.

The same thing can be done regarding the occupancy rate. Simply observe another restaurant for a month, and watch people as they come and go. How long did they stay? You can get a good idea. Now this is applicable for a restaurant business. For a software company or some other kind of startup, you may want to look at comparable data from similar startups so you have some basis for your assumptions.

If you have no basis for your assumptions, that is worrisome. You should be able to find some basis for making projections. One way to begin to make projections is to conduct interviews with people from similar companies, or perhaps ex-employees. That will give you some ideas, but it's an avenue that people often overlook.

Another great source of information concerning the assumptions that other companies have made is the S1 filing they must make when they go public. You can obtain these filings from www.10kwizard.com. This prospectus reveals all of the data from the beginning of the company. You can see for yourself the numbers a company was using for its financial assumptions. Then you can see what the actual numbers turned out to be.

Once you have done some research by looking at these documents, you will have a way to articulate the assumptions you are making. You will feel a lot more confident about your ability to make projections and run the company correctly.

You need to create an income statement with (annual) projections out to at least 5 years with revenue streams, expenses by departments, net income and ratios that compare your business with industry standards for the last year. No cute graphs, please. VCs want to see an actual Excel spreadsheet here.

Choosing KPIs

Everyone realizes the importance of key performance indicators (KPIs) in evaluating your business, but how do you choose which indicators to focus on? Each business is unique, and each will have different indicators. Here are a few things to think about when you are choosing KPIs for your company:

- Make sure the KPI relates closely to your company's goals. For example, if one of your goals is to establish long-term customer relationships, a good indicator might be the customer attrition rate. What percent of customers leave you each year?

Choosing KPIs
continued

- Make your KPI be essential to the success of your business. It can be the average order size per customer visit or the profit per customer visit. (Remember these choices will have a profound impact on how your business will be run, so chose them carefully.)

- Be sure your KPIs are measurable. "We're going to give the best customer service in the industry" isn't a measurable KPI. "Ninety percent of our customers do repeat business with us," is measurable and might be a good KPI.

Investors will examine your key performance indicators closely. Choose your KPIs wisely!

The Team

The team you put together must be compelling. It is extremely important, and you really have to demonstrate that it can perform. You must show that the members have worked together, gone through crises together. A team typically consists of two to three cofounders, plus strategic consultants and the advisory board. It also encompasses early employees. The kind of team you assemble will have a huge impact on determining whether you are investor-ready. If you are a solo founder with no team, I will tell you not to even bother approaching VCs, or probably even angels. Teams are extremely important.

Which is better, a great idea or a great team?

Of course, the answer to the above question is, "both." If you have a great team executing a great idea, your chances of being successful greatly increase. But I believe that it is much harder to develop a great team than it is to come up with a winning idea. That makes building a great team essential to your success.

Also keep in mind that your original idea will probably change and grow as your company develops. A great team will help you build that idea into something people will want.

Investors understand the importance of a great team. They are much more likely to fund you if you can demonstrate that your team is bright and creative and that you have worked through difficult situations together.

In addition to the eight points that we just reviewed, here are additional questions to consider as you try to become "investor-ready":

1) Do you have a compelling executive summary?

2) Do you have a short but compelling e-mail that your introducer can use to see if the investor is ready to see you or your executive summary?

3) Do you have a 10- to 15-slide presentation ready to show the investors? It should cover essential points and intrigue investors so they will want to meet with you for more in-depth discussions.

The processes of approaching investors will vary, but in general, you want to be introduced to an investor by something that they trust. Most of the time I send a compelling e-mail paragraph to see if they even have any interest in the space that the startup is working in. If there is interest, then I will send the two- to three-page executive summary and ask for a face-to-face meeting with a partner. I will ask the company founders to use this slide presentation to intrigue the investor during this meeting.

I will provide examples of executive summaries and sample presentations in the next section.

How much to raise in each stage

You always want to raise just enough capital to get to the next stage of development, or the next proof point as I call it, plus a little bit more to cover your expenses during the time it will take to raise the next round of funding. To put that in simple terms, when you are really starting your business, you will probably have little or no proof that markets need your product. You may not have any proof that people are willing to accept your pricing or your business model. You may have no proof that your team can work together. This situation represents a fairly large amount of risk for potential investors. You need to figure out how to get to the next proof point, where you can reduce or eliminate one or all of these risks.

Suppose that proof point is twelve months from now. Twelve months from now your product or service will be available in prototype form, and at least ten customers will have purchased it. That will give some proof that something is alive, that it's something people are willing to accept. Now you need to figure out how much money you are willing to raise to get to that proof point, plus six additional months. Why these additional six months? Because it will typically take you around six months to raise money for the next round. It may be shorter, or may be longer, but that is a good rule of thumb to have.

How much to raise in each stage
continued

This means that in our example, you should raise enough money to survive for eighteen months: twelve months to get to that next proof point, and six months to raise capital. The reason you don't want to raise all the money you will need is because your valuation at this stage will be low. If you raise too much money at this point, you will give up too much of the company to investors because there will be a lot of risk in the deal. You want to raise just enough money to get to the next level of risk or proof point. At that stage, the company valuation will go up, and you can raise a little bit more to get to the next proof point. And on and on it goes!

CHAPTER 6

Approaching and Engaging Investors

We have established the fact that the odds of getting funded are extremely low until you have traction. Sending a business plan by e-mail or handing them to investors in person is not advisable. Almost no VC is going to be swayed by the business plan you send them through their website. They get far too many such inquiries to look through each one. (Most of the VCs I know get around five hundred e-mails per day.) It is extremely hard for them to stay connected and current with everything people send them. Unless the e-mail is from a trusted partner, friend, business colleague, or a business company CEO, they may not even read it.

Who reads your business plan?

The answer to this question will shock you. No one! Nevertheless, the process of writing one is necessary for you to be able to write the executive summary that will be read by many. Both have the same 10 to 12 topics. The business plan addresses each topic in two- to five-page sections, while the executive summary covers the same topics in one paragraph each.

You have to find a more effective way to approach a VC. There are many ways to do it. The most common way involves being referred by someone the VC trusts. This might include a law firm or a business advisor. It might be someone who's done business with the VC before or the VC's former professor. Someone who has a previous relationship with the VC has a much better chance of getting his attention.

You also have to do some homework by studying the VC firm's website. Find out who the partners are, what they have done, and what companies they have invested in. You have to be completely prepared before approaching a VC. Most importantly, you must make sure that you have covered those eight items I talked about in the last chapter. Those items will help you identify the most important aspects of your business, so you can identify them for a VC.

The Art of Networking

Another good place to meet people who could refer you to a VC is through networking. If you are not networking frequently, you are unlikely to find people, whether you want them to join your team, become a founder in your company, or refer you to a VC. I recommend that you spend one night per week, or even as much as two or three nights per week, out at some event, on the internet attending a webinar, or at an industry conference where you'll be able to do some networking.

Networking is an art form. There is a whole method to how you find people, how you rub shoulders with them, and how you make networking connections.

The art of networking

You have to become slightly memorable to people before they will develop a rapport with you and, hopefully, refer you to a VC. I always tell my clients that they are not allowed to leave an event until they have collected at least five business cards and given away five business cards of their own. You also need to have conversations that are long enough that you can write one thing about that person on the back of his or her card.

It should be something that is not obvious from the card. It could be something they are passionate about, a hobby, or something that is going on in their lives. Maybe they are writing a book, or they're planning a trip to Malaysia. It could be anything. I want you to write one thing about them on the back of the card. Then, you should send them an invitation for LinkedIn, Facebook, or whatever your favorite method is for social networking. In addition, send them three touch points over the next three months. These three touch points could consist of almost anything related to what you wrote on the back of their card. Forward an article that is relevant to the conversation you had. Write a note saying, "I just saw an article that I thought you might find it interesting." Or, you could do some research about Malaysia, then write them a note: "I know you have been looking to go to Malaysia. I just put together a tip sheet, 'Five Things You Must See in Malaysia.'" Send something that will make them remember you and will show them that you did some kind of research after your meeting.

Know Your Tag Line

When you network, you must have a very crisp tag line virtually painted on your forehead. When people ask you what you do, it's your opportunity to tell them very specifically what you do and/or what you are asking for. You will be shocked! Doors will open for you that you never thought existed if you are able to communicate that information clearly.

Say, for example, that you are starting a software company. The last thing you want to do is meet somebody at a party or a networking event and, when they ask what you do, say "I'm in software." That is a completely generic answer. It is totally non-memorable. They may be curious and ask, "What kind of software?" But they may not ask any questions at all, which means you've wasted an opportunity.

Make a Lasting Impression

I find that people often say something like, "I'm in web technologies," or just, "Web 2.0." This is confusing and certainly not enough to make someone remember you. That again is an opportunity lost for a meaningful impression that could have been made. I would suggest you say something specific like, "I'm starting a company that provides online transaction security for the medical prescription market. People can order their medicines securely and in a way that is acceptable to most insurance companies."

Say something very specific, such as, "I am starting a company that is addressing the personal firewall problem for home networks, because a lot of people are downloading music and video. Our software specifically protects home firewalls so people don't have viruses entering their home network and compromising their security." An answer like this is much more likely to be remembered.

You can also add a commercial for your company and say "I am looking for a technical advisory board member who knows the Internet security market well." That little commercial after your introductory line is perfectly acceptable. You will be surprised by how valuable that can be in opening doors. If you don't tell people what you are looking for, there is no way they can help you. Every entrepreneur needs to have a crisp statement ready as he or she goes to a networking event. It's one way to attract the right response from the audience.

Presenting Your Company to the VCs

Most VCs do not require you to submit a business
plan in order to get a meeting with them. Instead,
they want to see a one- or two-page executive
summary that gives them a broad overview of your
idea, explaining what problem you are solving, how
your solution is different from that of other companies, who is on your team, your business model,
and how you plan to make money. This short business summary is all you need when you approach
VCs to convince them to meet with you.

Of course, you will have to write a business plan for
yourself in order for you to be able to extract the executive summary. At the very least, talk through all
the aspects of a business plan (even if you don't bother
to actually write it down), so you are clear about the
answers you need to give on your executive summary.

What Is in an Executive Summary?

The executive summary is the clear summation of
your business and your execution strategy. It gives
comfort and hope to interested investors, showing
them that there is money to be made, that you are
the one to make it for them, and how much money
they can make over time.

Your executive summary must be very compelling. It should be one page, ideally, and no more than three pages. In it, you answer some basic questions. The sections in your executive summary are exactly the same as those for your business plan. The typical sections are:

1) The problem you are trying to solve (the unmet need);
2) Market size;
3) Competitive analysis (How have other people tried to solve this problem?);
4) Your unique solution (Why and how will you be able to succeed?);
5) Business model (How will you make money?);
6) Go-to market strategy (How will you get your first ten customers?);
7) Key performance indicators and key financial assumptions;
8) Financial projections;
9) Team description and backgrounds;
10) A timeline or status, including what you have accomplished up to now and what you will do with the money you are trying to raise. Alternatively, you can describe how you will use the funds plus a timeline

that answers the questions regarding what you are planning to do in the next twelve to eighteen months and what you have done in the last six months.

Of course, the purpose of the executive summary is to get the VC interested enough in your startup to take that next step: invite you to make a presentation to the VC firm. This presentation is your chance to show these investors why they should invest in your startup.

How investors listen to you

Notice that we do not start our executive summary or business plan with "what we do." Most entrepreneurs start the conversation with any potential investor with this subject. I prefer by starting with "what problem we solve and who has this problem." This may be a subtle difference to some people, but it is an outside-looking-in conversation versus inside-looking-out issue. You have to approach the problem from an outsider's point of view. What is the problem that you solve, and is it big enough and interesting enough to be worth solving?

How investors listen to you
continued

Only once an investor is convinced of the fact that there is a big problem that must be solved will he or she want to understand how you are uniquely qualified to solve it and whether your proposed solution has potential. Once they can convince themselves of these facts and get over that hurdle, then they are interested in learning about your financials and go-to-market strategy.

VC Meeting & Presentation Preparation

At the VC meeting, you will make a presentation in which you will go through a lot of the information in your business summary, but in much greater detail. The meeting itself may be one hour, but you have to allow time for meeting and greeting, good–byes, and people running late. You also want to leave a good fifteen to twenty minutes for questions and answers, which will start sprinkling in very early in the meeting. You really do not have more than twenty minutes of presentation time.

You have to be fast on your feet

You may think that you have a one-hour meeting scheduled with the VC. In reality, you will get approximately twenty minutes to make your case. People may be late, time may be taken up with meeting and greeting, and there may be small talk. The VC may ask about your background or may want to tell you about their fund and philosophy. Don't get too comfortable! All this time is coming out of your one-hour meeting.

Control the timing. You will see people start getting up and leaving when the hour is up. They will also interrupt you almost from the get-go. VCs will ask you questions that you planned to cover in a later slide. Don't be deterred! Answer the question, and then address it with more details later.

Whatever you do, don't get flustered. Don't start flipping back and forth between dozens of slides, looking disorganized and confused. This could even be the VC's way of testing your ability to control a meeting. Be responsive and quick on your feet.

The Investor Pitch

It will be an important milestone for your startup when you are finally asked to make a presentation in front of an investor. Don't get too excited, though; you will have accomplished only 20% of the work in your quest to raise money. It is not uncommon to have to present to 30 or 40 investors before you find someone who is interested enough to pursue you.

But let's focus on this important meeting. You will be meeting the investors. I highly recommend that you stick with 10 to 12 slides to make your presentation. Under no condition should it be more than 15 slides. If your product requires a demo, you should include that time as part of your twenty minutes.

This is the kind of data your presentation needs to contain. I urge you to have your presentation reviewed by several advisors and professionals to make sure it is accurate, error-free, and written in a way that is easy to understand. You should also have another dozen or more "back-up" slides that contain additional material. They may be needed if the conversation demands it. But mostly, it will be the words coming out of your mouth that show your command of the market, intense customer knowledge, and passion for the idea.

VCs invest in people and markets.

How a VC Thinks While Listening to Your Pitch

Tips for Presenting to Investors

When it comes to your presentation, here are a few other tips. Have a simple and compelling presentation that can be given in less than 10 minutes. You don't have to tell them everything, just enough for them to fall in love. Make them want to know more. The best analogy is meeting somebody for the first time. Think of this as your "first date" with a particular VC.

Here is a suggested sequence of slides, each one with its intended purpose:

1) Who are we? (company description)—*This is what I call "slide zero" below.*

2) Why should you listen? (credibility)

3) What problem are we solving? (market)

4) How big is the problem? (market sizing)

5) How do we solve it? (solution)

6) What do we have to deliver? (product)

7) How do reach our customer? (distribution)

8) Is there money left at the end of the day? (unit economics)

9) What could go wrong? (competition, trends)

10) What will it look like when we run out of your money? (financial plan, milestones)

11) What's your level of interest? (trial close)

Expect to be thrown off while presenting to VCs. Don't freak out! It is only a test.

1. VCs are curious, smart, and impatient. They will ask a lot of questions when confused.

2. VCs are testing you:
   - Are you an effective leader?
   - Are you able to listen to "board room" feedback?
   - Are you able to listen to customer feedback?

3. Re-arrange the slide order to address issues that come up early

---

Keep Presentations Simple

Please do not have font overload. Stay with one simple-to-read font. You can use bold and underline to make points, but try to have more pictures, graphs, and diagrams, and fewer words. You also want to make sure you don't cram too many words in a single slide.

Guy Kawasaki's rule

The smallest font you are allowed to use on a slide is equal to the age of the oldest person in the room divided by two. If you are presenting to a bunch of forty and fifty year olds, the smallest font you should use is 24 (which is 48 divided by 2). You don't want to cram the page with too many words. You want to communicate the message with as few words as possible.

Remember, the purpose of pitching to VCs is simply to intrigue them so they invite you back for further discussion. Do not try to sell the whole concept in your first executive summary or your first presentation.

Presentation Style

You have to master these business communication techniques. Not just for raising money, and not just for career growth, but for the sake of your own personal relationships. Your PowerPoint slides are not the message—you are the message! You have to connect with your audience; you have to look in their eyes, and deliver your message.

A funding pitch should be like a mathematical proof. There are specific questions along the decision path for an investor. Make sure that each slide addresses one and only one question. When you present, please take notice of times when the investor does not buy in to what you are saying. Remember that you will not convince the investor of something new or challenging in a one-hour meeting. Take note of any objections, and address them later.

Even if the investor "gets" it, he or she has partners to convince of these points. Clarity counts.

Don't forget to pause

The most effective technique that I use in presentations is the strategic use of the pause. Long pauses really wake people up! Some presenters can't stop talking. If there is even a slight pause, they continue to talk and fill any space. Please do not do this. It is OK for the pause to linger. People need time to absorb the words coming out of your mouth. Give them a chance to do so.

Most of your audience is not going to remember many of the words coming out of your mouth, but they will remember your passion. They will re-member that last entrepreneur, the one who was genuinely excited about what he was talking about. Think about it: after listening to eleven boring pre-sentations, which one are they going to remember on Friday evening? The one delivered with passion.

Are they hearing you?

In order to connect with your audience, you need to make the message relevant to them in the first minute. Use pauses, dramatic tone, and energy while delivering your message. Practice your pitch on people you know. Set up a timer, and pitch to an audience of friends or colleagues. Tell them to write down what they heard. You will be shocked! What people hear is very different from what you are trying to communicate. I can honestly tell you I have done this several times, and the results are always rather shocking.

Do not read your slides. There is nothing more boring for the audience. VCs can read the slides themselves faster than you can do it for them. I always advise that the words that come out of your mouth supplement the data that is on the slide, not replicate it.

I suggest you use the title of each slide to deliver the message that you want the investors to remember. Just tell them in the slide title, and then the slide will provide data to substantiate the claim. For example, you may have a slide with the title "Market Size," and the slide has some charts and graphs on market size. How should you present it? I suggest that you change the title to, "Mobile SMS-based Advertising Market Growing at 84%" rather than just "Market Size." Give them the punch line in the title, and then use the slide to provide compelling data synthesized from your weeks of research to make the line convincing.

Slide Zero

You have to explain yourself during the first minute of your presentations. The first slide that's showing when you start talking typically has your company's name and your name on it. It may also have a tag line that tells the audience what your company does. That is it! I call this slide zero.

Investors must know which compartment of their brain they should open in order to store the words you are about to say. This is critical to getting the investors' attention. Slide zero is when there is nothing to distract. No chart, no graph, no bright colors, no moving objects. It's just the company name and you. Tell them what you do and why is it relevant. Tell the story. Tell the whole story. That stuff on your other slides should substantiate the story you tell on slide zero.

Example of a slide zero

There are many millions of gardeners in the USA. Not all of us live on a farm or with a patch of land for our garden. I love to grow things, but I don't know what can grow in my apartment on the thirty-second floor in Manhattan, and there is no one serving the needs of an "urban gardener." There is no place where urban gardeners can get together and learn from each other.

We are going to create a vertical social network for urban gardeners. Not only will they be able to learn, they will also be able to share their knowledge. It will be a ripe environment for advertisers. In the next fifteen minutes, you will find out how we will make money and how this company can become a go-to destination for the 5+ million urban gardeners who spend $1.4B per year on their hobby.

Tell the whole story. People often don't want to do that on slide zero. They think it's like a birthday party: I'm going to keep the surprise and slowly reveal my wonderful presentation over the next one hour! That is a risky move. Please explain the whole context on slide zero, so that the investor knows which compartment of his or her brain to store the information in. Tell your idea up front. People will get it.

SECTION III

The Funding Process

In this section, we will outline the process that an entrepreneur typically follows to seek funding and, hopefully, get funded. The process will vary from country to country and person to person, but I will lay out for you what typically happens in Silicon Valley. This example should serve as guidance for everyone, no matter where you are.

Investors anywhere in the world are essentially the same. They want to find good companies and entrepreneurs. They want to make more money. Your job is to provide them with as much supporting data as possible, so they can easily make the decision to fund you.

CHAPTER 7

The 12-Step Process of Getting Funded

I n this chapter, we will examine the process of trying to get funded. The funding process is slightly different for each of the funding sources we talked about in the last sections (angels, VCs, and strategic investors). In general, however, the entire process can be broken down into several parts. (The overall process is summarized in the flowchart below.)

As you can see in the diagram below, I have outlined 12 steps. You must pass through each to get to the next step. Each step can take weeks or months. It is not unreasonable for startups to spend four to twelve months raising money. This is why it is exhausting. It also explains why you must raise enough money so that you can run your business for twelve or more months, plus enough to run for an additional six months of fundraising. Otherwise, you are always in fundraising mode.

The one way to accelerate the process of getting funded is to be in the middle of a "bidding war." When there are multiple investors interested in your company, you can short cut most of this process. I have seen companies in this position get funded in as little as three weeks (although the average is probably six months).

The Process

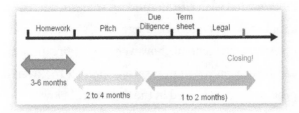

This diagram provides a high-level picture of the steps that you must go through to get funded and approximately how long the process should take. Below I will describe the 12 steps of the entire process and let you know what you should expect from each of these steps.

I have personally gone through all these steps on several occasions as I raised money for my companies. It looks daunting, but you can do it with the help of lawyers and advisors.

At the end of this chapter, I will also discuss two topics: how you know you are getting traction and how you can tell that investors are not likely to invest.

The 12 Steps to Getting Funded

1: Work on a business plan with your team
2: Extract info, create exec summary, 1-paragraph intro email
3: Get referred to investors, seek meeting
4: Conduct initial meeting, intrigue investors
5: Generate interest, seek follow-on meetings, repeat

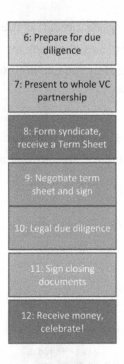

6: Prepare for due diligence

7: Present to whole VC partnership

8: Form syndicate, receive a Term Sheet

9: Negotiate term sheet and sign

10: Legal due diligence

11: Sign closing documents

12: Receive money, celebrate!

Get Referred

As I said earlier, it is very unlikely that you will send an unsolicited e-mail and get a positive response from an investor. You need to approach investors by doing research. Find out if you have a mutual friend or business partner who can refer you to one of them. The referral is a huge part of the process of getting funded. Of course, this also applies to almost any aspect of business. But it's especially true for investors.

If you can't find someone to refer you to the investors you want to meet, here's another option: try to meet them at an industry event. You may be able to get a few seconds of their time and interest them in scheduling a meeting with you. This has less chance of success than a referral, but if you can be charming and persuasive, you might be able to turn that few seconds into a meeting.

Let's start by focusing on the first steps of this 12-step process.

Steps 1 & 2: These steps can take from two to three months.

> 1: Work on a business plan with your team

> 2: Extract info, create exec summary, 1-paragraph intro email

What Do You Need to Send Investors?

As I discussed in an earlier chapter, the executive summary is the one document an investor is going to see when making a decision about whether to meet with you. That is why executive summaries are extremely important. You should put 80% of your effort for business plan creation into making an effective executive summary.

It's often harder to condense your business concept into a one-page summary than it is to write a long-winded business plan. It takes time to get your summary right so it resonates with investors. It doesn't happen overnight, which is one reason why it typically takes up to six months to get funding.

How investors evaluate your executive summary: a description of an investor's thought process

- Is the referral source credible?
- Is this company in my geography?
  - < 1 -2 hours travel time
- Is this a scalable business?
- Is the team credible?
- Are the existing investors credible?
- Can I possibly love the:
  - CEO
  - Target market
  - Problem being solved
  - Technology being developed

Fine-Tune Your Message

It will take you anywhere from a few weeks many months to find the right people, then to request a meeting by sending them an executive summary. Even if you get meetings, sometimes they will not be for another two weeks. You must not be impatient. It will take time. If you show desperation, it turns off investors. The best time to raise money is when you do not need it, or at least when you are not desperate. It is important that you take time to meet with your full list of potential investors, leaving time for you to refine your pitch.

I suggest that, at first, you approach five or six investors rather than all the potential investors on your list. Try to get five or six meetings. That way you can get an idea of whether your message is getting through to them. Once you have met with the first batch of five or six, fine-tune your message based on the weaknesses they may have identified. Then approach another five or six investors. After that, you can fine-tune your message even further. Keep repeating this process until your message is as strong as it can be.

Why an investor may not be Interested

- Partnership/partner is occupied with a "crisis" (that has nothing to do with you);

- Your sector is not considered "hot" by the investors;

- The investors or VC partners are not familiar with your market;

- The investors have lost money in your sector in the past (they are "burnt") and cannot look at it again;

- Your company is not in the right phase of maturity for the investors (either too early or too late);

- The VC fund life cycle does not match with what your company will need to mature.

The next three steps in our 12-step process of getting funded are listed below. These steps will take from two to six months, during which time most entrepreneurs get dejected and give up. This process is meant to weed out all but the most passionate and dedicated entrepreneurs.

3: Get referred to investors, seek meeting
4: Conduct initial meeting, intrigue investors
5: Generate interest, seek follow-on meetings, repeat

Approach Investors in Stages

I suggest that you approach your investor communications in stages. If you send the same initial
message to all 20 investors on your short list and
they reject your idea, then you have burned all
your bridges. It is very difficult to get back in the
door once it's been closed on you.

One thing to keep in mind is to not overshop the
deal. Overshopping occurs when everyone knows
that you are out looking for funding and, thus, may
be desperate. This is never a good sign. You should
carefully choose whom you want to approach and
why you want to approach them. Then you should
approach those investors in batches.

You want to start with a select subgroup of investors. Figure out if your story is making sense to
those investors, and then fine-tune the story and
go to the next batch of investors. Typically it takes
two to three months to get through the first one,
two, or three batches of investor conversations.
A typical scenario includes making a list of 20 investors who "should be interested" in your story.
Then, approach the first five, pitch to them, and
then fine-tune the story. Now you are ready to ap-

proach the next seven or eight investors. I usually put the most likely ones in this second batch. If no success comes out of these, then I turn to my third batch of investors. It may be smaller than the second tier, but it is still a good choice. If this list runs out, then I will start on my "B-list." This is the list that I work on as I go through my first list of 20 potential investors, and it is based on recommendations and suggestions by other investors that I am in the process of courting.

If any of those investors who are VCs show an interest, the next thing they will want you to do is talk to one or two other partners in their VC firm. You need to do this to build internal consensus among the VC partners. If more than one person in the firm likes what they hear from you, then the next step will be for you to meet with some of their "experts." These experts are people the investors know and trust, such as third parties within your industry. Sometimes they will be CEOs or management in companies they have already invested in. The investors want you to talk to them and get their independent opinion.

You, Under Scrutiny

Remember, investors are not only trying to validate the technology you are proposing; they are also trying to validate the kind of a person you are. This is a kind of a dance between you and the investor, and it can go on for weeks. During this time, investors are trying to feel you out while performing their own secret due diligence on you as a person, your market, and your technology. They want to know if you are patient. Do you get impatient with this run around? Are you able to work under stress, or do you fall apart after a while? Much of this dance is not technology-related due diligence. It's really about how you behave with them during this period.

It's almost like they are dating you. They are getting to know you slowly and trying to get comfortable with you. If their comfort level with you ever goes down, you could be ejected from the seat. They have such a deal flow and so many people coming to them that they have to be very judicious about how they spend their time. That's one reason why it's hard to get funded: you must get an OK from everyone you meet with at every stage in order to proceed further.

As you can imagine, when you are meeting with this many people, there can be considerable delay. Each meeting, whether it's with a single partner, several partners, or several experts, can take two to four weeks to schedule. This is in addition to the four months you can easily spend chasing down a VC who is sufficiently comfortable with you. So it really is a long process.

How can you tell when a VC is interested?

Let's say you start a meeting with one or two investors in the room. Midway through your presentation, they stop you and say, "Can you please hold on, let me see if Bob is in the building. I think that he would want to hear this." That is a good sign. I once started a one-hour presentation (the investor presentation that we discussed in the last chapter) during which three new people were brought in, one by one. That was a good sign.

If they like your story, they will reach out to you. If they are calling you to set up meetings and follow up, that is a good sign. You need to be responsive now. Get to work on any action item within 24 hours of your investor meeting.

Unlike angel investors, VCs, once comfortable with you and ready to go forward, will pull others into your funding opportunity. This is one interesting thing about VCs. Once they find a good deal, they almost always want to bring in someone from another firm to join them in forming a syndicate. They do this for several reasons. For one thing, having other VCs involved mitigates their risk. By involving another firm, they get another pair of eyes looking at the deal. Also, if the deal turns out to be good, then the other firm is likely to invite them to look at their good deals. VCs are a small fraternity and everyone really does know what everyone else is doing.

Once they begin putting a syndicate together, they will send you to three or four firms they would like to deal with. You will have to go through the same kind of process with these new VC firms (the process of pitching to them and getting them interested in and comfortable with you and your story) in your efforts to get them on board. That could take another month or two. It's not as long as the first period, but it still can be a long period of discussion and negotiation.

Steps 6 and 7 are next. Once you get through the previous steps, these steps can take from two to four weeks.

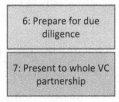

The Due Diligence Phase

During the due diligence phase, the VC firm will send somebody to spend one or two days with you and your team. This person will go through all the claims you made earlier. He or she will want to see how you arrived at your ideas about your market and your product readiness. This person will go through all of this information in excruciating detail. He will dig into your past like you won't believe and will find all of the documents about your invention, business plans, confidentiality agreements, and old contracts that you may have signed with your prior employer. He will want to talk to all of your employees and make sure you did not lie or exaggerate with any of your earlier claims. Only when the investors have done due diligence will the term sheet be discussed among the partners of the VC firm. I will talk more about term sheets later in this chapter.

Just as the investors, especially the VCs, want to conduct diligence on you and your team, you should feel equally compelled to conduct similar due diligence on them. You may not be able to demand stacks of documents from them, as they are likely to ask of you, but you should do some background checking and investigation. Talk to other companies that they funded in the past and talk to their CEOs and founders. It is OK to ask them for this information. Looking on the internet and making sure the investors are legitimate and have conducted their business ethically should also be a part of your due diligence process.

Due diligence is a two-way test drive

- Can I work with this team/VC for the next three to six years?
- Is this a quality team/VC?
- Does the team/VC listen?
- Is the team/VC honest, ethical, and reliable? Dependable?
- How do the team members react to being under fire?

You need to prepare for the due diligence phase. Here is your checklist of things to collect and do for the investors: (Prepare these documents, but do not send them. Wait for the investors to ask for specific items.)

1) Customer/technology references,
   a) Keep them updated on your progress,
   b) Use them judiciously;
2) Resumes & references for all founders, key employees, and executives
   a) Line up references in advance,
   b) Contact people VCs are likely to find on their own (e.g., your ex-manager who works as a VC);
3) Financial documents, including financial models, bank accounts, and ledgers;
4) Capitalization table (explaining who owns what percentage of your company);
5) List of all stock holders;
6) All confidentiality agreements and non-disclosure agreements;
7) All contracts and letters of intent that you've ever signed with anyone;
8) All consulting agreements that you've signed;
9) Documents used for creating the legal en-

tity for your new business and any legal filings with the government;

10) Any agreements that you signed with other companies to sell your product or to buy
products or services from them;

11) Any patent applications that have been filed;

12) A business plan.

The things that you should not have to provide as a
part of this due diligence process include:

1) Communications with other investors;

2) Unfiled patent applications;

3) Internal communications between founders, employees, and technologists;

4) Any communication between you and your
lawyers.

The process of getting funded will involve the following stages:

1) You will be asked to supply information
(exe-cutives' resumes, financials, cap table,
personal references, etc.);

2) You will be asked to meet with the VCs'
"experts," such as executives from their

portfolio companies, friends, and paid experts;

3) You will have additional follow-up meetings at your office and theirs;

4) Investors will make calls to customers and personal references;

5) Investors will also make calls to back-channel references (names that you did not supply but investors found on their own).

You have to be ready and responsive. Remember, they are also testing you to see how you are to work with. Will you be responsive over the next several years?

If you are lucky enough to make it through these stages, then you are among the one in a thousand entrepreneurs who can get to Steps 8 and 9. This process will take anywhere from two to four weeks.

> 8: Form syndicate, receive a Term Sheet

> 9: Negotiate term sheet and sign

Term Sheet

A few words about the term sheet (I cover term sheets in greater detail in the next chapter.): It usually comes up about five months into the process, if you are lucky enough to have investors talk about giving you a term sheet.

A term sheet is not a binding legal document. It is typically four to ten pages long, and it spells out the terms and conditions under which they may be willing to invest money. If you are seeing a term sheet, it is indeed good news. But it is by no means time to pop the champagne. A lot could still go wrong.

It's quite possible that you will be shocked at some of the terms that you did not expect, but remember that a term sheet is a nonbinding offer to invest and you will have room to negotiate a few terms.

Usually you will find that there are several terms that deal with liquidation preferences, voting rights, information rights, board composition, and several other factors that could be of great importance to you. After the term sheet is given to you, the investors will want you to sign it within two or three days. At this point, you need to get the advice of a qualified attorney with significant experience in venture transactions. Do not make the mistake I made and paid dearly for of hiring a cheaper divorce attorney. Get somebody lined up who has significant experience in startup and business term sheet experience.

The investors, their lawyer, and your lawyer will haggle out all kinds of terms and conditions. You want to get advice from your advisory board, as well as your attorney, to decide what is acceptable and what you want to get rid of. In the next chapter, we will talk about how to negotiate a term sheet. After the term sheet is signed, you may think it's finally time to celebrate, but no. You are not done yet—not until closing, when the money is in your account.

Before we go on to the specifics of the term sheet, I want to talk about two things: How do you know if you are getting traction from the VCs? How do you know when VCs are saying no?

Get Funded!   Section 3

How VCs say no

VCs in general hate to say no. VCs will be very positive and encouraging in a meeting and even when you follow up with them after the meeting. The reason for this is that they really gain nothing by telling you, "No," or "Your idea was no good," or "You were not well prepared." They never know. Tomorrow you may have a great idea, so they want to leave on a good note with you. They don't like to burn any bridges. That is why they almost never tell you no directly.

They usually have a subtle way of letting you know: they simply won't return your calls. Eventually, after several tries, you give up. If you can reach them, they will tell you polite things like, "We really love the team, but we are not investing in this segment right now," or, "We are over-weighted in this sub-sector."They tell you these things because they don't want to miss out on your future great idea.

My feeling is that you want to follow up with them and ask the questions, "If there is no interest right now, why not? What should the deal look like?" You can also ask, "What do you advise me to do in order to make my product more interesting to other investors?" They may give you some feedback; they may not. It depends on your relationship with the VC and how you ask.

Accept rejection gracefully and move on. Learn from what they told you. Be a very good listener and see what elements they had trouble swallowing. Get more data so that you can refine your pitch for the next VC.

How Do You Know You Are Seeing Interest from VCs?

Typically, when VCs are getting interested in making deals with you, you will know it. The VCs are making the calls that they promise they will make. They are making calls to introduce you to other people. After your presentation to a VC, you go back to your office and there is already a note from the VC about how the meeting went. Or, they quickly made e-mails or phone calls to some people they promised they would introduce you to.

If they are driving the deal, chasing you, you know there is traction. If you must chase them, that is usually not a good sign. I jokingly tell clients that you know the deal is going well when you go in to do your presentation to one person, and halfway through the meeting, he says, "Let me go grab another one of my colleagues." Before the meeting ends, you meet a couple of other people in the firm. That's a good sign.

A second sign that your deal has traction is a VC coaching you about how to present the idea to other people, either inside or outside the firm. When VCs become your coach, they are working on the same side of the table as you are. They have an emotional stake in the deal, and they want to sell it internally to their own colleagues. That is a sure sign that the deal is getting traction.

The next steps in your 12-step funding process are listed below. These should not take more than four weeks.

Once you have signed the term sheet, it is back to the original script. Now there will be legal due diligence. Earlier, you went through due diligence concerning your team and your technology. Legal due diligence deals, of course, with legal questions: Do you really have a properly formed corporation? Is it the right legal structure? Do you have any liens against you? Do you have any lawsuits or ugliness that should have been discovered earlier? If there are a lot of surprises during this time, a deal can easily be killed, and the term sheet made null and void.

The investors will also probably insist that you agree to what's known as a "No Shop Agreement." This means that once you have signed a term sheet, you are not allowed to talk to anybody else for 45 to 60 days. You will have to be careful that you don't violate that agreement. After you have gone down the path of legal due diligence and you have signed the proper papers regarding technology ownership, licensing agreements, and non-disclosure agreements, then the actual closing takes place.

The Closing

During the closing process, the actual money is transferred to your bank account. By that time you are usually so exhausted, frustrated, and on the edge that you don't feel like celebrating. But if you are going to celebrate, this is the time!

I have done half a dozen VC fundraisings in my life, and the process was exactly as I described, or slightly more painful. Several times, when I thought I was getting a term sheet, everything ground to a halt. Sometimes the reason can be due to you, such as some reference checks not working out the way they should have, but sometimes it has nothing to do with you. Instead, it can be related to the investors' internal affairs and the crises they may be facing in their other portfolio companies. I, myself, have had to start the process over again. Every time I have tried to raise money, it's taken me longer than six months to complete the process. It is hard and it is meant to separate the truly committed from the wannabe entrepreneurs.

CHAPTER 8

A Primer on
Term Sheets

Investors give you term sheets once they decide that they want to invest in your company. A term sheet is a document that is usually four to ten pages long. It spells out the terms and conditions under which the investors are willing to invest money in your company. It is a non-binding offer to invest that they can withdraw at any time—until you sign this term sheet.

It is a complex document. It may have over a dozen sections. Most entrepreneurs cannot figure out what is important and what is not that important. You are going to need the help of a lawyer in order to make sense out of it. But in order to simplify things, I want you to think about the term sheet as having four main parts that are important to understand.

1) Valuation: What your company is worth now (This will dictate percent ownership for you and your new investors.)
2) Exit math: Who gets what in an exit scenario
3) Governance: Board composition, veto rights, information rights
4) Founder's treatment: What bad things can happen to founders

You will have to negotiate a term sheet. You don't need to accept it as presented. But what items are important to negotiate? You may be surprised.

What should an entrepreneur care about in a term sheet?

Most entrepreneurs I know care about keeping majority ownership in their company and getting a high valuation. Valuation is the price that an investor places on the whole company prior to the new money coming in. That is why it is called "pre-money valuation." But I will show that valuation is not the most important aspect, and you should not confuse ownership with control.

Before we get deep into the term sheet, let's get one concept clear first. It is an important concept to understand when you are raising money: class of shares.

Common vs. Preferred Shares

One of the most important concepts to understand is the difference between two classes of shares in your company: common shares and preferred shares. Founders and employees get common shares. People who invest real money demand and get "preferred shares." They will insist on preferred shares, because preferred shares carry advantages with them: special rights that allow them to recoup their investment with a healthy reward.

Preferred shares are different from the shares you had when you started the company. Those are called common shares. While a company is private, investors want protection for their money from the risk. Preferred shares are their protection. I will explain how those protections work in a moment. The investors' "preferences" refer to their ability to take back money in case the company or its assets are sold and their antidilution rights that give them additional shares in case the future valuation of the company declines. These preferences also provide representation rights and the ability to chose and control the board of directors. I will explain all of these terms later in this chapter. For now, note that when a company goes public, all of those preferred shares convert to "common," meaning everybody gets common shares.

Stages of Funding

The first funding with professional investors results in your company issuing its first round of preferred shares, referred to as Series A Funding. Then comes the second round, known as Series B Funding, which is followed by Series C Funding. These funding levels represent certain levels of maturity for the company as well as classes of shares. Series A funding is used for product development, and initial traction with the first few customers. You raise Series B funding for product deployment, product validation, and for getting your initial sales up to a reasonable level.

You usually raise Series C for expansion capital. By this time (having spent money from Series A and Series B), you have a few customers, and you are going to expand to hundreds or thousands of customers. You need to set up sales channels, have promotions, and make alliances with other companies. That is what Series C funding is for. Series D is usually considered a late-stage investment, primarily used for regional or international expansion, getting established in a new business sector adjacent to your current one, or to rescue a company that is in trouble when Series C was not enough to get it to the stage where it should have been.

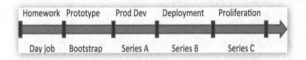

All of these Series A, B, or C preferred shares carry special privileges. These privileges are spelled out in the term sheet and the closing documents for each series of funding that you will close.

Let's analyze a typical term sheet with each of the sections.

1. Valuation

The first important aspect of getting funded is valuation. This will determine the percentage of the company you will keep as founders and what investors get. Valuation is the current value of the company. For investors to come up with a stock

price at which they will invest money, they have
to come up with a valuation for the company. You
may have your own thoughts about what the company is worth. But investors will do their own calculations and come up with a number based on
their comparables. They need to be able to justify
the valuation to their limited partners. Valuation is
an important number, but it is not the most important thing to focus on.

The valuation will be expressed as, "We propose
to invest an aggregate of $X million, representing
a Y% ownership position on a fully diluted basis,
including shares reserved for the employee option
pool as set forth below." Or the term sheet may say,
"We propose to put 3 million shares of the Series
A preferred stock at a price of $1.00 per share."
If you had 4 million shares prior to this funding,
then this sentence implies that the company was
valued at $4 million by the investors (pre-money
valuation) and that after the closing of funding, the
post-money valuation will be $7 million. This also
implies that the investors will own three-sevenths
of your company post-funding (approximately 43%
ownership).

Aim for an "Up Round"

Many entrepreneurs get hung up on the valuation. In reality, there are other things that are far more important than the valuation. Allow me to introduce you to what you <u>should</u> be paying attention to: whether your company's valuation is rising. Good things happen to a company when its valuation goes up in each subsequent round of funding. When your valuation increases in a round of funding, it's called an up round.

Suppose your company was valued at four million dollars, and an investor added three million. Your post-funding valuation is seven million. Two years later, when you're raising the next round of funding, if the valuation is above the $7 million mark, then it is an up round. Hopefully, after one or two years of execution, you have done significant work, which has raised the valuation.

If this is the case, you are in good shape. You can negotiate and establish the pre-money valuation on the next round at $11 million. In that round, you raised another $6 million, which brought the post-money valuation to $17 million. Then one or two years later, when you are raising money again, you ideally want the valuation to be higher than $17 million. This is an example of what it means to experience up rounds. Everything is fine when the rounds are up. You are happy and your investors are happy.

The Down Round

Really bad things begin to happen when you have a down round. A down round means the pre-money valuation for the next round of funding is less than the post-money valuation of the last round. Most term sheets contain clauses designed to protect investors when down rounds happen. When down rounds happen, it means you screwed up. Or, maybe it was not your fault. Maybe market conditions were really bad during that period. In reality, there might be many reasons for the down round. The fact is, investors don't care. All they care about is the fact that the company is worth less than when they last touched it.

Investors Protect Themselves in Down Rounds

Term sheets have all kinds of clauses that are triggered after down rounds to protect investors' interests. Who gets screwed? The entrepreneurs. The founders. This is one reason that you don't want to start with a very high valuation. If your valuation

is too high at the end of a funding round, you may
have trouble achieving a higher pre-money valuation the next time around. If you start with reasonable numbers, you have a better chance of having
an up round the next time around.

You want to avoid having a down round at all costs.
That's when bad things happen. You should be
more worried about down rounds than about your
company not getting a valuation that's too low. I
know many examples of companies that were very
happy to receive a very high valuation—but it came
back to haunt them later.

2. Exit Math: Who Gets What in an Exit Scenario

This is a very important section. This determines
who gets what when the company has an exit. The
exit is when investors cash in. It can be an IPO
(Initial Public Offering) when the company stock is
listed on a stock exchange. It can also be a merger,
or acquisition by another company.

When there is an IPO, then all is well. All preferred
shares get converted to common, and all shareholders are treated equally. The trouble starts when

there is an acquisition or a merger. Liquidation preferences guarantee that preferred shareholders will get their contributed capital (sometimes multiple of what they invested) before any common shareholders (read "the founders") get any money.

Some of the things that preferred shareholders get are:

1) Liquidation preferences that allows them to get their investment out first before anyone else gets their hands on the money, in the event of the company (or its assets) being sold or acquired;

2) Antidilution clauses that protect them in case the company valuation drops in subsequent rounds of funding;

3) Information rights that allow them to get financial information about the company on a periodical basis;

4) Veto rights that allow them to control the sale of stock to another party or sale of the company.

Liquidation Preferences

Liquidation preferences spell out what happens when companies have a liquidity event (otherwise defined as an "exit"), such as a merger or acquisition, or a public offering of the company's stock. These preferences tell you who gets what.

How Liquidation Preferences Work

You need to know the value of the liquidation preferences in your term sheet. It could be 1X, 2X, or 3X or even higher. Here's what that means: when a liquidity event happens, the investors get their money back first. If they have a 1X liquidation preference, they get the same amount that they put in. If they have a 2X preference, they get twice the amount they put in, and so on. Sometimes you even hear of a 3X or higher liquidation preference.

Let me give you an example of how this can affect you. Suppose investors put in $10 million. Your company was sold for $50 million. You own 10% of the company, so you see yourself getting five million dollars from that sale. Maybe not! Suppose the investors had a 3X liquidation preference. They get their initial $10 million back, and since they had 3X liquidation preference, they get

an additional $20 million. If they had another
clause which paid them an 8% dividend per year,
suddenly their $30 million becomes $32.4 million
if the acquisition happened three years after they
invested. (Dividends of 8% on a $10M invested
capital results in $800K per year dividends.) Now
there's only $17.6 million left. If they had "partici-
pating preferred shares" (another term that you
may find in the term sheet that allows investors to
double dip), they can convert the preferred shares
into common shares after collecting their preferences. Then they can participate along with you
to divvy up the remaining $17.6 million.

If you had 10% of the company, you are getting 10%
of $17.6 million that remains after investors took
the first $32.4 million. Your economics could dra-
matically change, depending on the kind of liquidation preference terms that were in the clauses.

Good investors, in reasonable times, get 1X liquidation preferences. If the investors in this example
had a 1X preference, they would have taken their
$10 million back, plus the 8% dividend. They would
have taken about $13 million. Then they would
have converted their preferred shares into com-

mon shares. At that point, you would be dividing the $50 million minus the investor's $13 million, $37 million total. Your portion would have been $3.7 million. You can see how much difference liquidation preferences can make. That is why it's so important to understand liquidation preferences and negotiate those, instead of worrying about valuation. Valuation is important but not that critical.

Antidilution
Antidilution clauses are also important. Some investors will insist on terms that will issue them additional shares in the future in case a future round of funding is at a lower valuation than the current round (called a "down round"). This type of antidilution clause is called "full ratchet" and can significantly hurt the founders, as they do not get any such protection and can see their ownership erode dramatically.

3. Governance
The third bucket in the term sheet is governance. Governance deals with board seats, control, information rights, and veto rights.

Governance covers issues like how many board seats investors will control, what kind of control you will have, and what kind of control the investors will have. It has to do with voting rights and the kinds of things that can be voted on. For example, it's common to have a term that a founder cannot block the sale of a company. If the board decides to sell, the founders can't keep it from happening. This may or may not be acceptable to you.

What is a Typical Scenario?

Typically, Series A investors will want to rearrange the board. If you have advisors or family members or all of the founders on the board, it will be changed. Series A investors tend to take two board seats, the founders representing the interest of all common stockholders will have two seats, and a fifth seat will be reserved for an independent person. This person can be a professor or some person with unique knowledge of technology or markets. It is sometimes negotiable whether this fifth person will be chosen by the mutual consent of the investors and the founder or just by the investors. Your founding team may need to have a discussion about who is best for the board. If an outside CEO needs to be brought in, it is possible that he or she will take one of the two seats being reserved for common stockholders. This may mean that only one seat remains for a founder.

One way to address losing a board seat is to offer some people the status of Board Observer. This means they get to attend all of the meetings and receive all of the investor communication, but they do not get to vote. For angel investors, early investors, or founders, this can be a suitable compromise for relinquishing their board seats.

You should not have to offer compensation to any board members except the outside independent members. Compensation is usually in the form of some modest stock options vesting over a period of time. Cash is not involved until much later, once the company reaches profitability.

In subsequent rounds of funding, new investors will demand another board seat. The new term sheet may expand the board to seven people as new investors are added.

There will also be information rights. This covers questions like how often you have to give status updates or send a financial statement to investors.

Are the financial statements only for investors who have at least $50,000 invested in the company, or for all investors? This issue of information rights is important because you may have several small shareholders, and even some employees, who don't need that information. You don't want everybody who ever held your stock to have information rights. Many terms fall under the category of good governance. You want to negotiate these terms to make sure you get a fair deal. Board control is probably the most important issue you will face. I will talk more about the makeup of your board in the next chapter.

4. Founder's Treatment

The fourth bucket has to do with how founders are treated. This part of the term sheet is the most important, at least in my opinion.

Term sheets usually spell out what happens when founders have to be replaced or fired. What happens to their stock? What happens to their severance or salary? All these things are usually spelled out in the term sheet.

Stock vesting

Stock vesting is something that usually creeps up in negotiations late. Founders may be placed under a vesting schedule. Let's say you started a company, and you own two million shares. Investors may demand that these shares be subject to a four-year vesting, meaning that you can keep your shares only if you stick around for four years. Otherwise, the company has the right to buy them back from you. You may find this appalling, but it is normal. From the investors' point of view, they are investing in YOU. What good does it do them if you walk away 12 months after they funded you? They want your head in the game. Stock vesting is their only leverage point.

I recommend that you accept this, but get the investors to make some concessions. You may have them start the clock when you started the company so you are seen as being already 25% vested as of today; then the vesting period will be an additional three years instead of the normal four. You may also be able to negotiate some clauses stating that if they kick you out, you get all your unvested shares immediately vested (or at least most of them). Vesting is not pleasant, but you don't have much leverage, unless you manage to get multiple term sheets!

Stock vesting

continued

Remember, every time you negotiate, you need to have leverage. If you only have a single term sheet, your only leverage is to walk away. If you have multiple term sheets from different investors, you have leverage to negotiate better terms.

You should know how you will be treated in case of a termination. Will you get to keep your stock? You started the company, the investors forced you to vest your stock over four years, and then investors fire you after eleven months. Are you left with zero stocks after all the effort you put in? That would not be fair. This is your time to negotiate a fair agreement.

You should also define exactly what "getting terminated" means. Suppose the board does not terminate you, but they demote you from president to director of marketing. That may be unacceptable. The various ways that investors can remove you from power should be covered in a clause called constructive termination.

There are multiple clauses that should be discussed with the investors:

1) Termination without cause;
2) Termination with cause (and then you must agree on a definition for "cause");
3) Constructive termination.

Termination With Cause

There may also be language in the term sheet dealing with termination with cause and termination without cause. In the case of termination with cause, you should have "cause" clearly defined. You must negotiate all these items before you sign the term sheet. Otherwise, you are at the mercy of investors, trusting that they won't wrongly terminate you. Use a lawyer who specializes in startups and dealing with VCs to advise you. A typical definition of *cause* would be your having been involved in some illegal activity, such as fraud or employee harassment, or convicted of a felony. You should define as narrow a scope for "cause" as possible with the help of an attorney.

Constructive Termination

Good investors invest in you, and getting rid of you is the last issue they want to deal with; but sometimes, it is in the best interest of the shareholders. The Board (now controlled by investors) has different ways of forcing you out, without actually firing you. They might assign you to the office in India for a few years. That may not be an attractive assignment for your family! Also, your salary might be dramatically reduced for no reason. Any of these things, and more, can be considered *constructive termination*. If this occurs, you want to make sure you can accelerate your stock vesting accordingly. ("Accelerate" means being able to own more, even all, of your options now—as if the time has accelerated—even if your original vesting period has not passed.)

Change in Control

Another section of the term sheet has to do with change in control, or what happens when the company is acquired. What happens to your stock then? Do you accelerate? You need to spell out the conditions under which your stock will accelerate. This is a likely scenario if you succeed. You may get acquired, and you will want to know what happens

to your stock and what your severance package
will be if you are terminated after the acquisition.
This is the best time to negotiate these terms.

Single trigger or double trigger?

The terms single trigger and double trigger apply when
there is change in control (usually defined as more than
50% of the company stock changing hands), in other
words, when your company is acquired by another entity
or a merger takes place. A single trigger occurs when a
company experiences a change in control. If the company
gets acquired AND your position is terminated (or significantly altered), it is a double trigger. You may be able to
negotiate what will happen to you in case this happens.

Investors will insist that they pay you any special
payouts or accelerate your vesting only if a double
trigger happens. Double trigger refers to two conditions happening one after another, for example,
a change in control, followed by your getting de-
moted within 12 months, or getting fired in less
than so many months after the transaction. As you
can see, a double trigger is less likely to happen.
This is why investors want this.

It is customary and reasonable to have a double trigger, but please pay attention to the definition of termination. Be sure to include "constructive termination" in that definition.

In these situations, you can demand some accelerated vesting of your unvested stock (perhaps six to eighteen months of acceleration in the vesting schedule) and some severance payment (perhaps three to six months of salary and benefits). If you can negotiate more than this, it is of course better for you.

How to Negotiate a Term Sheet

These are the four sets of topics of discussion that you need to look for inside a term sheet. These are the items you want to negotiate. Negotiating a term sheet is an art form in itself, and you will need to use your lawyer's help.

Ideally, your startup is so compelling that you should have more than one term sheet so that you can have leverage while negotiating. If you only have one term sheet, then you can still make a list of the issues that are most important to you and, with the help of your lawyer, approach investors on the three, four, or five issues you want to discuss.

If you walk up to them with a list of 23 items, it will not look good and they will start to wonder what it will be like to work with you over the long period of time ahead. You have to choose your battles and hope for the best. Terms sheets are meant to protect the investors when things go bad. If the company succeeds as planned, most of the terms in your term sheet will never be triggered.

Negotiating a term sheet is not much different from negotiating a prenuptial agreement. You have to contemplate all the bad things that could happen. Don't over-negotiate to the point where all parties have a bad taste in their mouths; you will have to work closely with these investors as a part of your Board of Directors.

Finding a good lawyer

Is there a particular type or size of law firm that is best for you? The answer is no. There are advantages to working with large legal firms. They have a wide array of resources that can help you navigate the funding waters. But large firms are typically more expensive. Smaller firms are usually cheaper, and you get more personalized service. But they don't have the same resources within the firm that a larger firm has.

Finding a good lawyer
continued

The best way to find a lawyer that can help you negotiate terms with a VC is through referral. Ask your friends and colleagues that have been through the process who they used. Find out which lawyers have a good reputation, and which ones should be avoided.

You are much more likely to find a good lawyer through recommendation than by hunting on your own. But, even when lawyers are recommended to you, be sure to interview them for yourself. Make sure they are the right choice for you.

(I have much more information on the legal side of start-ups in a book I wrote called *The Definitive Fast-Start Guide to Lawyers*. It's available at http://fivemountainpress. com/books.html)

Don't Over-Negotiate; Be Professional.

You don't want to negotiate every issue in the term sheet. Figure out three or four items that are most important to you, the areas where you want to take a strong position. You will look like an amateur if you try to negotiate all twenty-three or twenty-four items. That will make the process far too long.

If investors are not fully excited about the company and you decide to negotiate every point on the term sheet, this may just tip them over the edge and make them say forget it. If investors think you are going to be difficult, they won't take the time to deal with you. They would rather just move on and invest in a different company.

This is a complex subject to cover as one chapter in a book. I have provided you with a few salient points that will help you in being smarter when and if you get to the stage of finally getting a term sheet in your hand. It should open the door to further reading and study on your part once you are in that lucky group of people who receive term sheets.

CHAPTER 9

Post-funding Priorities

After you receive funding, there is a whole set of issues and rules about board composition, investor communications, and your interaction with the board. I have a separate book on the life of a founder/CEO that deals with this in a lot more detail. But here I will just give some highlights. Once you have a board, it is vital that you earn its members' respect and trust.

Running Your Company

When you are just starting a company, you may think that raising money is the hard part. In fact, it is only a small part of the entrepreneurial experience. Your real work is still ahead of you. Resist the temptation to start spending money and change your frugal style. Money is oxygen, and you are stuck in a mine. You must conserve every ounce of this oxygen.

This is make-or-break time. You should work with a finance person to set up a budget and track every penny. You must always know how much cash is left and what your fume date is (that is, the date the money runs out if nothing else comes in). You should have strategies in place to extend this fume date if needed.

Extend Your Lifeline!

There are several ways of extending your funding and, hence, your lifeline. You may have the ability to seek venture debt from a business bank. Banks often extend lines of credit to companies that are venture funded, without any collateral. (This is sometimes referred to as "venture debt" because using these lines of credit actually puts you in debt to the bank.) The banks take a small piece of equity for this privilege and charge you a hefty interest rate. But these lines of credit can be very valuable if you must extend your runway for a few months in order to meet a deadline before you seek the next round of funding.

These credit lines have significant risks, so use them only if you must. The banks do not provide risk capital. They do not like risk. If there is any sign of trouble, these banks will demand their money back, and that can often trigger a cash crisis. I have used these venture debt lines successfully, but I have also lost companies because of them.

Set Up Processes That Help You Track Performance

In order to run the company, it is very important to set up key performance metrics. Remember, your actions will set the tone for how things are done, especially in the early days when there are no written procedures. This is how you set the company culture. Begin by doing things the right way, and you will have a much greater chance to be successful.

Board Relationship and Management

After you receive funding, there is a whole set of issues and rules about board composition, investor communications, and your interaction with the board.

Your Relationship with the Board of Directors

Board trust is extremely important. The first thing to remember is that you have to be open and honest. Never lie to the members of your board. If you say you are going to do something, do it. Also, remember to keep things very organized. Send them a packet of information that contains the issues you plan to discuss with them 48 hours before the meeting. Give them a chance to absorb it. Come prepared to every board meeting.

Schedule a year's worth of board meetings at the beginning of the year. Make sure people can reserve and block those dates. I usually suggest having eight board meetings per year. But some investors will insist on meeting more often, perhaps monthly. Board meetings are your chance to communicate to the board that you are in control. They want to know you are on top of the same issues they are worried about. They want to know about your plan of action for the most pressing issues facing the company.

How Often to Approach Board Members

You also want to meet with each board member once between board meetings. One-on-one over lunch is the best way to do it. This is just to hear them out, to give them a chance to address the issues that are on their mind.

One thing that is different about being a CEO is that suddenly you have multiple bosses. Each board member is technically your boss. You thought your life was hard when you had one boss in your previous job! Now you will have four, five, or six bosses, and each one of them will be hard to please. But, your honesty and integrity will earn their respect. This can be a very profitable and exciting partnership.

A few words of caution: you don't want to over-communicate with the board. Keep in mind that you want to give the board good news, as often as you can. You can give good news via e-mail, but bad news should always be given face-to-face.

Running Board Meetings

It's also important to remember that you should never surprise your board. Never bring up bad news in a group setting. When there is bad news, ideally, you should have talked to each board member, either face-to-face or by phone, before the meeting. Give them the news ahead of time, so when they come to the board meeting, every-one has heard the news. You don't want it to be a big shock. If you surprise the board with bad news during meetings, your days as a CEO could be numbered. Nothing will cause you to lose a board's confidence faster.

This is one reason why CEOs need a coach or an advisor. They need at least one person that they can be completely open with at all times. You cannot run to the board with every thought that comes to your mind. You will become very annoying. You need some other person, preferably a coach, that you can interact with, to help you synthesize your thoughts before you approach the board. (This is just a helpful tip, based on my own experiences.)

CHAPTER 10

What If You Don't Get Funded?

If you don't get funded despite months of trying, don't give up. This is something that will happen more often than you think. Reflect on your assumptions. Do you still really believe in your idea?

You may go back to the drawing board and refine your idea, pick a different approach or segment to focus on, or change your business models. It is also OK to give up. Sometimes this process reveals to you that you really did not have that much passion for the idea or the life of an entrepreneur. This is OK too. You may return to this startup business later, when you are in a different stage of your life or have found stellar cofounders or have gained more knowledge.

You may determine that you have done enough research and you want to bootstrap the company until
it becomes profitable. (In some businesses, you can
get to a point of profitability by bootstrapping it.)
Once you are profitable, many more doors open to
you. The best way to approach an investor is to be
able to say, "Look, Mr. Investor. I am getting so many
orders they are falling on the floor. I have no time
to pick them up. Would you give me some money
to hire people to process these orders?" That is the
ideal scenario.

I realize that doesn't really happen, and I'm being funny. But this is close to what many investors
need to hear. That is a true example of traction.
If you are not close to that, then you need to ask
yourself if it is really worth pursuing. When do you
know it's time to quit?

This is one of the hardest decisions you will make as
an entrepreneur. Here's the truth: you must give this
decision your full thought process and do all the research I have asked you to do. Once you've come to
the clear realization that this not going to work, it's
time to ask for the opinions of your advisors, people
you trust. If three people who are not related to you

say it's time to move on, then you probably should listen to them. You should move on.

Are You Doomed?

Remember: After you unburden yourself from your previous startup, all the knowledge and experience is still in your head. You will probably be a lot more successful starting the business a second time around. It may not be in the same field or with the same idea, but the knowledge you have acquired as an entrepreneur in the process of starting a company is valuable tuition that you have paid. That knowledge will stay with you.

I always think of it this way: I have paid tuition—or in some cases, someone else (an investor) has paid the tuition—for my learning, and I am a better, more experienced person going forward. Another thing I advise you to do is to keep a diary and remember the mistakes you made, the things you never want to do again. Also, keep a log of the things you want to do better and differently next time. If you keep a journal like this, you will be surprised at how valuable it is when you do go to the second stage in your life, whether your startup was successful or not.

Failure isn't final!

Milton Hershey. H. J. Heinz. Henry Ford. Walt Disney. Mark Zucker-berg. All people we know today as leaders in their particular industries, innovators, titans. But most people don't realize they also share something else in common: each one of these people led businesses that failed before they found success.

They didn't succeed because they hit on the perfect idea the first time. They succeeded because they kept going, even after they failed. If your first startup fails to get funding, it doesn't mean you should never try again. It might just mean you need to learn from your mistakes and move forward to the next opportunity!

Alternatives

Remember, there are other alternatives for getting funding, even if you don't get money from angels and VCs. They are slow. They take a long time, which is why I did not include them in this book earlier. But they are worth mentioning in this chapter.

Consider something called SBIR (Small Business Invest-ment Research) Grants in the U.S.A. Each federal government department has some percentage of their budget allocated for grants for research projects. These grants are typically $100,000 for the first phase. The second phase can be as much as $500,000.

They are given to entrepreneurs who are doing research or working on some relevant product in an area the department is working in. All agencies, from NASA to the Department of Energy and the Department of Defense, give money to SBIR Grant holders. It's a long application process. It may take several months to apply. You must make sure all your "I"'s are dotted and your "T"'s crossed, in order to get the money. But many entrepreneurs do successfully use them. I urge you to look into this option, and consider getting some of this government money.

In U.S., you should also look into an SBA (Small Business Administration) loan. SBA does give out loans to entrepreneurs. (Governments in other countries give out similar loans, under different names.) These loans may be forgiven if you don't succeed, or paid off at a favorable rate. They can give you the necessary capital to prove out your business and try to get it to a profitable stage.

Technology or Company Sale

When you come to the understanding that it's going to be hard to go forward with your startup, it is time to consider selling the assets of the company. This could mean selling the technology, the intellectual assets of the company, the patent application or patents, or even the whole company. You should utilize strategic advisors to help you with this decision.

There are companies that specialize in the sales of companies, and/or intellectual property. They will normally take a hefty commission. Their cut may be ten, twenty, thirty, or even forty percent, to help you make the transaction. It may be a time to explore such options. There is probably somebody, a competitor perhaps, who has an interest in what you are doing. Sometimes, you'll have a situation where Company A may already have a product similar to what you are designing, but they may be interested in buying your technology for defensive purposes, so Company B does not acquire it and try to compete with Company A.

I urge you to explore those moves. When you come to the realization that it is time to move on, you may want to contact the most senior person available at a company that may want to acquire your startup. Some could be competitors; some could be in your competitive landscape. Approach them with honesty, saying, "I have tried this and I haven't been able to succeed for these reasons. I know this technology has value. Perhaps it will find more use inside your organization."

There is a whole art to selling a company. The right way to sell technology to a company is the topic of a future e-book. Even if you have given your best try and you are not able to get your company funded, there are options for you to try. Perhaps you can get some money back and monetize. Or maybe you can get some stock options back at another company, if you are able to get more out of it.

CHAPTER 11

Final Advice

The questions that I am asked most often by entrepreneurs deal with investors and how to get your venture funded. The topic is so vast that there is no way to cover all that I have learned in my life, but I hope that this book has been valuable to you. I have raised over $100M from all the sources that I have listed in this book. I am hopeful that I have provided some guidance, and shed some light on, how you may approach investors. I hope your probability of success has gone up.

Getting funded is hard. Do not give up. You will find yourself refining your thoughts and presentation after a few pitches to investors. This is normal. As you get more comfortable with your presentation, acquire more intense customer knowledge, and are able to articulate an investment thesis, you will get better at fundraising.

Remember, if an investor takes a pass, it does not necessarily mean that your idea did not have merit. It could mean several things: perhaps their investment thesis du jour does not match with what you are trying to do. Maybe the timing is wrong for them, or they don't have expertise internally to judge or guide you as an investor. Perhaps they have already made too many investments in this subsector and do not want to be overweight. It could simply be that from three companies they can fund, the other two look more attractive on a relative scale. It does not mean that your company is not a great investment for another investor.

Here is a checklist that your investors have on their mind for you. Your job is to help them check off each item through your interactions with them.

1) Is there any potential to grow fast?
2) Is the market big enough to build a big company?
3) Is there room in the market for this start-up?

4) Is the market big enough to maneuver if the first niche doesn't work out?

5) Does the team really know the customers?

6) Is there a logical reason behind the customer list?

7) Is this list of potential customers strategic or opportunistic?

8) Is there any notion of customer segmentation?

9) Are the customers Tier-1?

10) How much are the customers helping?

11) Does every team member demonstrate success? What is the company pedigree: have team members worked as market leaders? Have they had personal success?

12) Do they have a startup mentality, or a big company mentality?

13) Have the entrepreneurs passed a rigorous background check?

14) Is this product a "feature" or a "company"?

15) Can the incumbent (current competitor) add this feature to an existing product easily?

16) Can the value proposition create a substantial business?

17) If the revenue forecast does not materialize, can the company still survive?

18) Is the revenue projection too big, too small,

or just about right?

19) Has the spending plan been scrutinized?

20) Are these entrepreneurs frugal?

I have never been able to raise money with less than 20 pitches to different investors. It is a numbers game. You should not feel bad about getting rejected.

It may not be you! It may be "them" after all.

I would like to hear from you about your own experiences. I invite you to send me your stories, ask new questions, and share your thoughts. These can help me to enhance this book and will allow me to write about new ways that we all can benefit from each other.

Naeem Zafar
Silicon Valley, CA
Summer 2010.

Appendices

Example of an Executive Summary
Template from www.bandangels.com

Logo

Pain:

Solution:

Newco, Inc.
Address :
Phone:
Fax:
Website:

Basic Details:

Founded In:
Of Employees: 15 (X US / Y offshore)

Funding History:

Total Amount Raised to Date:

Total Seeking: $

Committed Funds (If Any):

Use of funds: E

Valuation Expectations:

Financials:

Cumulative Revenue:
Burn Rate: $
Cash Flow Positive in: Year ?

3-Year Revenue Forecast:

Year 1: $
Year 2: $
Year 3: $

Team:

- *Company founded _____*
- *_____ Patents filed on _____*
- *Product Introduction _____*
- *$ in sales in x*
- *$ in sales in x+1*
- *$ in sales in x + 2*

Resources for Entrepreneurs

♦ **Law Firm Outreach**

   ♦ DLA Piper Venture Pipeline

   ♦ www.venturepipeline.com

   ♦ Fenwick & West LLP

   ♦ Orrick, Herrington & Sutcliffe LLPs "Total Access"

   ♦ Pillsbury Winthrop Shaw Pittman LLPs "Back Stage Pass"

   ♦ Wilson, Sonsini, Goodrich, and Rosati wsgr.com/WSGR/Display.aspx?SectionName =practice/venturecapital.htm

♦ **National Association of VCs is a great source. Get a full listing of all VCs at** http://www.nvca. org/ (it has 430 names of VCs—click on the "members" under "About NVCA" tab).

♦ National **Association of Angel Investors is also a good resource for entrepreneurs. See** http://www. angelcapitalassociation.org/entrepreneurs/.

♦ www.TechCrunch.com is a **good blogger's site.**

♦ www.Entrepreneur.com **is a good source of varied information for entrepreneurs.**

♦ www.TheFunded.com, **for user-generated comments on VCs and investors.**

♦ www.Inc.com **is a good resource for many things entrepreneurs need.**

+ www.Go4Funding.com **has a list of and links
  to websites for angel investors.**
+ http://venturehacks.com/angellist is another
  list of angel investors with links.
+ *SVASE, Silicon Valley Association of Startup
  Entrepreneurs*: www.svase.org
+ *The Enterprise Network of Silicon Valley*:
  www.Tensv.org
+ **Women's Technology Cluster:** *www.wtc-sf.org*
+ **Entrepreneur's networks**
  + The Indus Entrepreneurs www.TIE.org and
    www.tiesv.org
  + www.OPENSiliconValley.org

List of VCs

VC	LOCATION
Azure Capital Partners	San Francisco, CA
Bain Capital	Boston, MA
Band of Angels	Menlo Park, CA
Battelle Ventures	Princeton, NJ
Battery Ventures, L.P.	Waltham, MA
Bay Partners	Menlo Park, CA
BBH Brown Brothers Harriman & Co	New York, NY
Ben Franklin Technology Partners of Central and Northern PA	University Park, PA
Ben Franklin Technology Partners of Northeastern PA	Bethlehem, PA
Ben Franklin Technology Partners Southeastern PA	Philadelphia, PA
Ben Franklin Technology Partners Southeastern PA	Philadelphia, PA
Benchmark Capital	Menlo Park, CA
Bessemer Venture Partners	Larchmont, NY
BioVentures Investors	Cambridge, MA
Brook Venture Partners LLC	Wakefield, MA
BV Capital	San Francisco, CA
Canaan Partners	Westport, CT
Catamount Ventures, L.P.	San Francisco, CA
Charles River Ventures	Waltham, MA
ChevronTexaco Technology Ventures LLC	Houston, TX
Chrysalis Ventures	Louisville, KY
CIT GAP Fund	Herndon, VA
Claritas Capital LLC	Nashville, TN
Clearstone Venture Partners	Santa Monica, CA
CMEA Ventures	San Francisco, CA
CommonAngels	Lexington, MA
Connecticut Innovations, Inc.	Rocky Hill, CT
DCM Doll Capital Management	Menlo Park, CA
De Novo Ventures	Palo Alto, CA
Delphi Ventures	Menlo Park, CA

VC	LOCATION
DFJ Element, L.P.	Radnor, PA
DFJ Frontier	Santa Barbara, CA
DFJ Mercury	Houston, TX
Domain Associates LLC	Princeton, NJ
Draper Fisher Jurvetson	Menlo Park, CA
Draper Richards, L.P.	San Francisco, CA
Duff Ackerman & Goodrich LLC	San Francisco, CA
Easton Hunt Capital Partners, L.P.	New York, NY
eCoast Angels	Portsmouth, NH
Edison Venture Fund	Lawrenceville, NJ
El Dorado Ventures	Menlo Park, CA
Emergence Capital Partners, L.L.C.	San Mateo, CA
Envest Ventures	VA Beach, VA
Essex Woodlands Health Ventures	New York, NY
Expansion Capital Partners LLC	San Francisco, CA
Felicis Ventures	San Francisco, CA
First Round Capital	West Conshohocken, PA
Forward Ventures	San Diego, CA
Foundation Capital	Menlo Park, CA
Foundation Medical Partners	Rowayton, CT
Frazier Healthcare and Technology Ventures	Seattle, WA
Gabriel Venture Partners	Redwood Shores, CA
General Catalyst Partners	Cambridge, MA
Globespan Capital Partners	Boston, MA
Goldman, Sachs & Co.	New York, NY
Granite Global Ventures	Menlo Park, CA
Greenmont Capital Partners, LLC	Boulder, CO
Greycroft Partners	New York, NY
Greylock Partners	Waltham, MA
HarbourVest Partners LLC	Boston, MA
Harris & Harris Group, Inc.	New York, NY
HealthCare Ventures LLC	Cambridge, MA
Highland Capital Partners LLC	Lexington, MA
Highway 12 Ventures	Boise, ID

VC	LOCATION
Hummer Winblad Venture Partners	San Francisco, CA
IDG Ventures Boston	Boston, MA
Ignition Partners	Bellevue, WA
Illinois Ventures LLC	Chicago, IL
Innovation Works, Inc.	Pittsburgh, PA
Insight Venture Partners	New York, NY
Intel Capital	Santa Clara, CA
InterWest Partners	Menlo Park, CA
Investor Growth Capital, Inc.	New York, NY
Ivy Capital Partners	Montvale, NJ
JMI Equity	Baltimore, MD
JumpStart, Inc.	Cleveland, OH
Kansas Technology Enterprise Corporation	Topeka, KS
Khosla Ventures	Menlo Park, CA
Kleiner Perkins Caufield & Byers	Menlo Park, CA
Labrador Ventures	Palo Alto, CA
Lacuna, LLC	Boulder, CO
LFE Capital	Minneapolis, MN
Lightspeed Venture Partners	Menlo Park, CA
Longworth Venture Partners, L.P.	Waltham, MA
Lovett Miller & Co. Incorporated	Jacksonville, FL
Madrona Venture Group	Seattle, WA
Maryland DBED	Baltimore, MD
Maryland Technology Development Corporation	Columbia, MD
Matrix Partners	Waltham, MA
Mayfield Fund	Menlo Park, CA
Meakem Becker Venture Capital	Sewickley, PA
Menlo Ventures	Menlo Park, CA
Milestone Venture Partners	New York, NY
Mission Ventures	San Diego, CA
Mohr Davidow Ventures	Menlo Park, CA
Morgenthaler Ventures	Menlo Park, CA
MTDC Massachusetts Technology Development Corp.	Boston, MA
New Enterprise Associates	Baltimore, MD

VC	LOCATION
New Jersey Economic Development Authority	Trenton, NJ
New Leaf Venture Partners, LLC	New York, NY
New Science Ventures, LLC	New York, NY
NextStage Capital	Audubon, PA
NGEN Partners LLC	Santa Barbara, CA
NGP Natural Gas Partners	Irving, TX
North Bridge Venture Partners	Waltham, MA
North Hill Ventures	Boston, MA
Norwest Venture Partners	Palo Alto, CA
Novak Biddle Venture Partners, L.P.	Bethesda, MD
Nth Power	San Francisco, CA
Oak Investment Partners	Westport, CT
OCA Venture Partners	Chicago, IL
OpenView Venture Partners	Boston, MA
O'Reilly Alpha Tech Ventures, LLC	San Francisco, CA
OVP Venture Partners	Kirkland, WA
Oxford Bioscience Partners	Boston, MA
Palo Alto Investors	Palo Alto, CA
Peninsula Equity Partners	Menlo Park, CA
Pequot Capital Management, Inc.	Westport, CT
Pequot Capital Management, Inc.	Westport, CT
Plymouth Venture Partners	Ann Arbor, MI
Polaris Venture Partners	Waltham, MA
Prism Venture Partners	Westwood, MA
ProQuest Investments	Princeton, NJ
Psilos Group Managers, LLC	New York, NY
PTV Sciences	Houston, TX
RAIN Source Capital, Inc.	Saint Paul, MN
Redpoint Ventures	Menlo Park, CA
Rho Ventures	New York, NY
RRE Ventures LLC	New York, NY
Rustic Canyon Partners	Santa Monica, CA
Safeguard Scientifics, Inc.	Wayne, PA
Second Avenue Partners	Seattle, WA
Sequel Venture Partners	Boulder, CO
Sequoia Capital	Menlo Park, CA
Sevin Rosen Funds	Dallas, TX

VC	LOCATION
Shasta Ventures Management LLC	Menlo Park, CA
Sierra Ventures	Menlo Park, CA
Sigma Partners	Menlo Park, CA
Signal Lake Management LLC	Westport, CT
Sofinnova Ventures	San Francisco, CA
Spark Capital	Boston, MA
Stata Venture Partners	Dover, MA
Steamboat Ventures	Burbank, CA
Stonehenge Capital Company	Baton Rouge, LA
Storm Ventures	Menlo Park, CA
Summit Partners	Boston, MA
SunAmerica Ventures	Los Angeles, CA
SV Life Sciences Advisers	Boston, MA
TD Capital Ventures	Boston, MA
Tech Coast Angels, Inc.	Los Angeles, CA
Three Arch Partners	Portola Valley, CA
Trident Capital	Palo Alto, CA
Trinity Ventures	Menlo Park, CA
True Ventures	Palo Alto, CA
Tudor Ventures	Boston, MA
Tugboat Ventures	Menlo Park, CA
U.S. Venture Partners	Menlo Park, CA
Union Square Ventures	New York, NY
Updata Partners	Reston, VA
VantagePoint Venture Partners	San Bruno, CA
Venrock Associates	New York, NY
Venrock Associates	New York, NY
Verge	Albuquerque, NM
Versant Ventures	Menlo Park, CA
Village Ventures	Williamstown, MA
Voyager Capital	Seattle, WA
vSpring Capital	Salt Lake City, UT
Weston Presidio	Boston, MA

List of Angel Investors

Active Angel Investors
Alliance of Angels
Angel Capital Network
Angel Healthcare
Investors
Angel Investor Forum
Angels Corner
Angels Forum
Arizona Angels
Atlanta Technology
Angels
Atlantis Group, LLC
Aurora Angels
Band of Angels
BarryMoltz.com
Ben Franklin Technology
Partners
Ben Franklin Venture
Investment Forum
Bio Cross roads
Bi-State Investment
Group
Blue Angel Ventures
Blue Ridge
Entrepreneurial
Council
Blue Tree Allied Angels
Boise Angel Alliance
Business Development
Company of RI
CA Investment Network
Camino Real Angels
Centennial Investors

Charleston Angel
Partners
Chesapeake Emerging
Opportunities Club
Cincinnati's Angel Capital
Hub
CommonAngels
CoreNetwork
CTEK
Delta Angel Group
Desert Angels
Desert Frost Ventures
First Run Angel Group
Florida Angel Investors
GAIN Innovation
Network
Gathering of Angels
Golden Gate Angels
Investment Group
Grand Angels
Great Lakes
Heartland Angels
Houston Angel Network
Hub Angels Investment
Group
i2E, Inc
Idealflow Angel Fund
Inception Micro Angel
Fund
Innovation Works
Investor's Circle
Jump Start
Keiretsu Forum

Kohler Center for
  Entrepreneurship
Boston Harbor Angels
Launchpad Venture
  Group
Life Science Angels
Lore Associates
Louisiana Angel Network
Maine Angels
Maverick Angels
Midwest Venture Alliance
Nashville Capital
  Network
NCIC Capital Fund
New Jersey Angel
  Network
New Mexico Angels, Inc
New Mexico Private
  Investors
New Vantage Active
  Angel group
New York Angels, Inc
North Bay Angels
North Country Angels
North Dallas Investment
  Group
Ohio Tech Angel Fund
Oregon Entrepreneurs
  Network
Pasadena Angels
Phillips Nizer
Piedmont Angel Network
Portland Angel Network
Richmond Venture
  Forum

River Valley Investors
Robin Hood Ventures
Rockies Venture Club
Sacramento Angels
Sand Hill Angels
Seraph Capital Forum
Sierra Angels
Silicom Ventures
Silicon Pastures
Springboard Capital
Startup Florida
Tech Angel Fund
Tech Coast Angels
Tech Valley Angel
  Network
Technology Alliance
Tenex Medical Investors
The Angel People
The Angels' Forum
Tri-State Private Investors
  Network
Utah Angels
Vancouver Autodesk
  Inventor Group
Virginia Active Angel
  Network
Walnut Venture
  Associates
Westlake Securities
Winter Park Angels
Women Inventing Next
Women's Venture Fund
Jersey Angels

Naeem Zafar

Naeem Zafar is a member of the faculty of Haas Business School at the University of California, Berkeley, where he teaches Entrepreneurship and Innovation as part of the MBA program. He has also lectured on business, innovation, and entrepreneurship in India, China, Japan, Singapore, Turkey, and Pakistan. He was invited to the Presidential Summit on Entrepreneurship in Washington, DC, and frequently travels for the U.S. State Department to speak on the topics of entrepreneurship.

Naeem is a serial entrepreneur, having started his own business at the age of 26 and gone on to start or work at six other startups. He has extensive experience as a mentor and coach to entrepreneurs and CEOs, and is the founder of Concordia

Ventures, a company that educates and advises entrepreneurs and startups on all aspects of starting and running a business.

Naeem most recently served as president and CEO of Pyxis Technology Inc., a company specializing in advanced chip design software for nanometer technology. He has also been president and CEO of two other technology startups, Silicon Design Systems and Veridicom (a Bell Labs spinoff that invented the silicon fingerprint sensors today found on most laptops). Naeem has held senior marketing and engineering positions at several companies, including Quickturn Design Systems, which had an IPO in 1993 and grew to $125M in revenues.

Naeem obtained a Bachelor of Science degree (*magna cum laude*) in electrical engineering from Brown University in Rhode Island, and he also has a master's degree in electrical engineering from the University of Minnesota.

Naeem is a charter member of TiE (The Indus Entrepre-neurs, www.TiE.org) and a charter member of OPEN (www.OPENSiliconValley.org), where he serves as the president. Naeem has served on the board of directors or advisory board of 25 companies. As a part of his global entrepreneurial practice, he is involved with microfinance ventures and social entrepreneurship.

Naeem's experience in starting his own businesses, as well as advising hundreds of entrepreneurs and dozens of startups, puts him in a unique position to help others succeed.

To contact Naeem about this book or his strategic advisory service, e-mail him at naeem@startup-advisor.com.

Several other e-books by Naeem Zafar are in the works. Please sign up at www.startup-advisor.com so that you can be notified of new e-books relating to entrepreneurship.

Please look at www.FiveMountainPress.com to purchase other e-books being published by this author.

Printed in the USA
CPSIA information can be obtained
at www.ICGtesting.com
CBHW032354210724
11940CB00005B/32